A TRUE STORY BY
ANTONIO A. FELIZ

OUT OF THE BISHOP'S CLOSET

a call to heal ourselves,
each other, and our world

Published by Aurora Press, San Francisco, California

Library of Congress Cataloging in Publication Number
88-71560

Feliz, Antonio A.
OUT OF THE BISHOP'S CLOSET
a call to heal ourselves,
each other, and our world

1. Church Work With Homosexuals
2. A.I.D.S.
3. Mormons

I. Title.

ISBN 0-929582-00-4

Dedication

To my children, whom I love as their father. No matter where life's sure changes take us, my love for them I keep within. It is true, constant, abiding and unbounded by geography, philosophy or cultural differences; my love for my children will not be stopped by death nor by any other kind of separation.

Acknowledgements

There are many people to whom I am deeply grateful for their unique contributions to the publication of this book. In most cases, however, these must remain anonymous, and I acknowledge that they are the reason for its publication.

As far as specific acknowledgments are concerned, I want to make it known that my sweet mother has been the perfect Mom—that she has always so been—throughout the painful writing of the manuscript.

Of all those who have encouraged and provided hope as the final stages of publication came, Bill Nelson is the one who was there when the need was greatest, and I am deeply grateful. Also, Pete Kouris of Electronic Yearbook Photography Company of America and co-founder of television's The Weather Channel, is another who's contributions made this book possible.

I am thankful for the work and kind assistance of historians and other stewards of historical documentation at the Church Offices of The Church of Jesus Christ of Latter-day Saints and to those at the Historical Commission of the Reorganized Church of Jesus Christ of Latter Day Saints. Their respective contributions are inestimable.

Without the special abilities of AFFIRMATION GAY AND LESBIAN MORMONS, I would not be alive today to write my story. It is these faithful saints who have provided me with an unavoidable determination to publish. I have witnessed their courage and an inspiring faith in the face of their unique and insurmountable odds.

I am very grateful for the cooperative assistance I received from Sandra McDonald in the preparation of the manuscript for printing. I will always remember her dedication to this project, even in a series of persecutions from neighbors claiming to be Christian.

Without the generous and freely given contributions of Wayne Snider, David L. Burnett of Global Moon Press, and others who cannot be mentioned here, along with Jerry, Leon, Ron, Jon, and David, this book could not have been published.

Where errors or misrepresentations seem to exist, they are unintentional. If these exist, they are my own and do not have their origin with anyone else.

Antonio A. Feliz
June, 1988

Note to the Reader

This is a true story. Its publication is not intended in anyway to deride, defame or to show disrespect. As you read on, please understand that much is taken from my personal journals and, as such, is now written with the emotion and flavor of the moment in which it was originally written. Retaining the wording as it was originally written, hopefully, preserves for the reader the flavor of what I've experienced. However, in order to protect the privacy of certain individuals and especially because I know we are all merely imperfect humans, after all, the names of most persons have been changed. With one exception, the names of persons considered public figures have remained as they are in actuality. Also, some of the incidents are combinations of more than one incident. However, I have done all that I know how to ensure that what is herein written is true and factual to the best of my memory.

The Author

Contents

Contents

Our heavenly Father is more liberal in His views, and boundless in His mercies and blessings, than we are ready to believe or receive.

Joseph Smith Junior
August 27, 1842
Teachings of The Prophet Joseph Smith, p. 257

Preface

Joseph Smith said in his *Lectures On Faith* that Christ "...was exposed to more powerful contradictions than any man can be." This book is about contradictions. It is about theological and social contradictions and paradoxes in my own life. This is my story. I was ordained to minister for God and found myself caught in the contradictions of the official teachings of my church. As with any true story about personal struggles with things Divine, it is a story of love and healing in the midst of an ego-centered world, a world caught in the warp of disease.

This book is also about AIDS. It is an articulation of one person's perception of the true reason for the existence of AIDS in our society today.

In Eastern thought, koans are usually stated paradoxes. These statements are often enigmatic, illogical gibberish at first glance. Our rational, Western mind tries to dismiss them and move on. However, a Zen master carefully picks a koan for a student and requires that the student contemplate on the statement and then respond. A student normally tries ever so dutifully to make sense of the koan and...fails. At that moment, the moment of giving up, the student will spontaneously achieve some influx of what Mormons would call "Pure Intelligence." The Zen master would call it receiving enlightenment. Important to this Zen practice is the fact that while the new insight may not seem to relate with the koan, the koan was the vehicle that brought about its perception and articulation. I believe that our struggle with AIDS is such a koan for our society today.

Thus, this book is for Catholics, Mormons, Protestants, Jews, and all others who strive to be "spiritually minded" persons. Those who relate most with the fact that they are either Gay or Lesbian who have had a religious upbringing, will especially relate well with experiences in this story. And, even though it is written in the context of a Mormon Bishop's experience, the issues I have had to deal with are universal issues that find themselves in all paternalistic religious movements.

However, this book is of significant importance for those who are not either Gay or Lesbian, but who for various reasons, have had this issue impact on their personal lives. To Latter Day Saints in this group, I sense a need to direct some specific prefacing comments:

Most Mormons learn in their high school years about "higher law." This is a plea to allow higher law to operate here. Allow the higher laws of "faith" and "love" to operate. These two higher laws (or principles) are actually powers (or principles of power) which elevate and exalt us as we apply them. My hope is that we may all become more faithful and more loving as a result of this story.

Any questioning of a familiar moral standard or ethic can feel extremely frightening to a person who truly desires to live a godly life. But, ponder for a moment that perhaps one reason why church leaders do not wish to consider the theological implications of this subject openly is because of these desires to live as godly a life as possible. I sincerely believe that is a good reason to be shy about this subject.

While my individual spiritual journey forced me to examine traditional Mormon beliefs in "eternal increase," I now can see that the paradox of eternal increase and homosexuality are actually placed here as a koan for us to see things as Joseph Smith would have had us see them. My plea, therefore, is that the reader proceed with an open mind, tolerating the fear that may accompany this exploration and believe and trust that the doctrines of exaltation and eternal increase (as taught by Joseph Smith) are not under attack here. Allow love to cover fear.

My personal story is a story of discovery. It is a story of finding the core problem that doesn't allow a very natural part of me to fit into the grand puzzle of today's accepted doctrines. My experiences forced me to face this problem directly. My perspective was one of an ecclesiastical leader as well as one that came from being the object of today's cultural scorns. I was literally forced into confrontation. I would see things in light of official church policy, through the reality of my personal experience, and they simply did not compute. I was searching for harmony and experienced piercing disharmony. For me, my entire life had become what a Zen master would call a koan.

As a Western thinker, in my relatively unintuitive way, I had been led by my mind. I'd tended to build foundations out of traditions, teachings or theologies in order to feel secure. I would believe that I knew of the truth of a belief because it was logical or because I needed it to be. Today, I see that it is only when I let go of these traditional concepts that I was able to see the core principles of truth that Joseph Smith was trying to teach the saints of his day.

In brief, this book is about one person's experience in letting go. It's about the development of an ability to function without the encumberances of traditional theology that contradict personal realities. But, it's also about the development of an ability to function in an abundant fashion, not just to bear the burden of life's uncertainties It's about joyfully learning from life's inconsistencies, including its uncertainties.

Difficult though it may be, I trust you'll continue reading. As you read what I have written in love about love, may those higher principles of faith and love—which empower and exalt us—be your Sure Guide.

The Author
June, 1988

In order to lead them to bliss,
God lays on those whom He loves
something that is not blameworthy
in His own sight, but for which
the world will criticize and blame
them.

Saint Juliana of Norwich
REVELATIONS OF DIVINE LOVE
Chapter 28.

Chapter 1
Personal Dichotomies

"HOLINESS TO THE LORD." The familiar words greeted me as I prepared to enter the temple in Los Angeles, California. It was the autumn of 1973 and the temple was solemn and majestic against the blue California sky. This holy edifice truly was for me a place where heaven and earth met, a window through which I personally could step into heaven. A young couple would kneel before me today at one of the altars in this place that was so sacred to me, and with the power that had been given to me through a Prophet of God, I would seal them to each other for the rest of their eternal lives. I had the power spoken of in the scriptures. According to the belief of my Church, I had been given that power to bind on earth in such a way that those I sealed to each other could be together not only in this place and time but in all places and times: Marriage for Eternity, unique to our belief in some respects, but so common a desire throughout the human family. I was the agent. As always, the weight of it was heavy on me. But today, somehow that weight was even heavier than usual.

What presumption is it in us that lets us think we can act for God? Who was I to exercise such a power as this? To speak for God? To act in God's place? I knew I had the power. It wasn't that. I had stood often enough in that place and had my mind opened to know exactly what it was a particular man and woman needed to hear, needed to know and remember as they began their life together. I knew how close heaven and

1

earth really were. But today, I felt strangely unworthy to use that power. I sought assurance. I needed to feel again, as I'd felt before, that I really was worthy to do what I was going into the House of The Lord to do.

I changed to my white clothing. It was some time before the ceremony was to begin. The carpeted hallways softened my steps as the noise of the world began to recede. These walls protected me. The distractions, the rush were left behind. I checked the necessary paper work. Everything was in order. I needed to be alone. I climbed the massive circular staircase to the upper chambers of the temple. It encircled the huge chandelier around which this spiral took my steps. At the top, I stopped and looked down below me at the brightness of the thousands of lights in the chandelier hanging in the center of the spiral of stairs. Beauty filled the hollow shaft which I'd just climbed. I went on. Where could I go to be alone? The serenity of this place was around me as I passed the Terrestrial Room, a wonderful place of light and growing things where a large group was gathered. I entered the Celestial Room of the temple. Here was our effort to create a place that was as much like heaven as we mortals could imagine. A place where God could come. The large room was empty. I walked slowly around it. The adjoining hallways and sealing rooms were likewise unoccupied. I chose a chair and sat down, trying to focus my troubled thoughts. In this beautiful and sacred place of peace my mind was not at rest. The more I tried to clear my mind, the worse it was. I couldn't.

Today especially, I needed to feel that God heard me. In my mind, I addressed him as one would speak to another person. "God, Father, let me know you hear me." I still felt very much alone. I took a deep breath and clasped my hands in my lap, and I tried to let go of my connection to earth.

I had tried all my life to do what God wanted me to do. I'd consecrated my time and talents and all I'd been blessed with to the building up of the kingdom of God on earth. I'd been a missionary in South America, preaching for two years at my own expense, because I wanted others, everyone, in fact, to know what I knew and feel what I felt. I'd been a Bishopric Counselor and High Councilor. I'd blessed many people through those callings. Somehow I felt the need to remind God of that now. Why should I be feeling what I was feeling today when I had tried so hard to do what I felt God wanted me to do. I'd tried to be the man God wanted me to be.

The room was quiet. The peace of the place began to filter into me. I felt a gentle reminder that as the Branch President of the Spanish-speaking branch in Los Angeles, I had the right to seek guidance concerning the needs of those saints. But it was I who needed guidance today.

Three days before, I had been required to hold a Church court for a young man in my congregation who had been accused of living in a homosexual relationship with his roommate. "No unclean thing can enter into the kingdom of God," we'd been taught. It was my responsibility to determine if Sergio would be allowed to remain a part of the Church, or be cast out. The memory of the "trial," as ominous and weighty as any physical burden, would not leave me...

* * * * * * *

"Sergio" I'd asked gently in Spanish, "do you understand the seriousness of the charge against you?"

He shrugged his bent shoulders, but didn't look up at me.

I tried again. "We want to hear your side, Sergio. Tell us what happened."

He raised his gaze hesitantly to meet mine and I saw how his dark eyes were full of tears he was struggling to hold back. I waited for him to speak.

"Yes," he said at last. "It's true what you say of me. I do love another man. And I know you say it's wrong for me to love him in this way." He paused. "I want to do what's right, President." He said it as if he were afraid we wouldn't believe him. I believed him.

"But it doesn't feel wrong to me! Aren't you supposed to be able to feel it when things are wrong? Can't we tell?"

"Then tell us how it did make you feel," I prompted.

"Sometimes I'm afraid," he said. "Sometimes I feel so alone. Sometimes I think no one will ever love me. Then he puts his arms around me. He holds my body close to his. He makes me part of him." We waited until he was ready to go on. "Then, then it's all right. He loves me. He holds me. We love each other. How can it be wrong to love someone?" He was pleading with us to see it his way. I wanted to. I didn't want to condemn him. I felt the same need to be loved, to be held, to be made whole. He had faced us with courage. A courage I lacked. He'd shared his deepest feelings. Mine remained unspoken.

I had to ask the next question. The part of me that loved my Church and my God wanted to ask it sincerely, but the words did not come easily. "You've taken the first step, Sergio, in coming to us and confessing your sins. Are you now willing to forsake them and make your life right with the Lord?"

He looked at me steadily without answering, and though there was no condemnation in his look, I felt he somehow knew more about me than almost anyone else. That he knew exactly what I'd been feeling as he described his lover's touch and the warmth of his friend's body close to his. Finally, his eyes still locked to mine, he shook his head slowly. "No," he said. "No, I guess I'm not willing to do that."

We invited him to leave the room for a few minutes and I asked my two counselors for their impressions. "He's not sorry," one said. "He's not the least bit repentant. For his own good, we have no option but excommunication." I knew they were right, but I didn't want them to be right. Why should people be condemned because they were honest? I was the one who had sat there in silence. I felt torn.

Sergio rejoined us. I pronounced the verdict. At the word "excommunication," a kind of stubborn defiance replaced the hesitancy with which he'd spoken before. With his hands outstretched, as if he would grab me and shake the truth

4

Personal Dichotomies

into me if he had to, he said, almost spitting out the words in his anger and frustration, "President Feliz, aren't you ever going to learn that there are other ways of looking at things? I tell you, the Church is wrong on this one! Why can't you see that?"

I had no answer.

* * * * * * *

What would it like to be touched intimately by a man? In the quiet of the temple, my turbulent thoughts would not be still. To be hugged sensuously, even kissed tenderly by another man, and to return those intimate sensual responses?

I forced the thought away. No! It was wrong to feel that way. It was wrong to want that. It was a sin even to think about it. I knew that. I tried to pray again.

"Heavenly Father," I began silently. "I'm married to a beautiful and sweet woman who loves me and loves you..." Laura's face came into my mind. So serious, so sincere, so concerned whenever she sensed a strain between us. How I'd prayed and fasted and prayed again before I'd proposed to her, begging the Lord to bless me with the ability to love a woman so that I could marry and have children and learn to fill the measure of my creation. And what wonder it had been when I'd finally felt it. And I did love her. Didn't I? I'd been sealed to her. We'd knelt across from each other at the altar, our hands clasped, and had been promised that if we were true and faithful, we would be companions in Eternity. But then why, why couldn't I feel for her what I'd felt for...other faces blurred with hers...

Terry. Being near him in the early morning seminary class we'd shared as teenagers, the strength of my incomprehensible desire to touch him and be close to him had simply bewildered me. I remembered the morning after class when Terry looked at me with that same desire; how he'd touched me and how that had called out yearnings for him from deep within me. I remembered how much I'd yearned for his look, his touch.

5

Then Ken. He'd pulled me innocently into his sleeping bag one freezing night so we could keep each other warm as we tried to fall asleep in the back of his pickup on our way to Salt Lake for conference. He'd been so warm next to me. I'd felt so guilty enjoying the closeness of his warm body.

Other faces came to my memory, faces of other guys to whom I'd felt attracted in my teen years. Were they all infatuations in a stage, a part of youth?

I tried to repeat the prayer I'd prayed then. The prayer I sometimes felt I'd been praying ever since. "Please, God, take these feelings away from me. I want to love my wife. Keep me strong. Don't let me do anything I shouldn't. Please."

But I felt totally alone. Abandoned even. Pulled and stretched in too many directions. Laura. Terry. Ken. Sergio, and others. Unanswered questions hammered at me, relentless and demanding. "Please, God. Please." I realized I was crying. I reached for my handkerchief to dry my face.

Just like Sergio, I wanted to do what was right. I wanted desperately to do what was right. I knew that the men who led the Church were inspired. And if they said that what I was feeling was wrong, then it must be. I wanted to follow them.

I had decided when I was sixteen that I needed to know for myself if David O. McKay, then President of the Church, really was a Prophet of God. Somehow I knew that if I went to Salt Lake City for a General Conference of the Church, I'd find some way to meet this man and, when I did, I'd know if he really did speak for God.

The memory of that experience has never left me; it probably never will...

****

Temple Square glowed in the spring sunshine. Ken's parents were saving our seats in the Tabernacle balcony as he and I went out to get a newspaper before the conference session started. In the warmth of the sun lit April morning, it

6

was hard to believe that only two days before, Ken and I had been caught in a snowstorm in central Utah and spent the night huddled together in one sleeping bag in the back of his truck trying to keep warm. We hadn't done anything but hold each other to keep warm, but the guilt surrounded me like a dark cloud, blocking out the glory of the morning.

As Ken and I walked around the Tabernacle, a large, grey limousine drove past us and parked near the west doors of the Tabernacle. For some reason, I froze at the sight of it, but Ken ran right up to the rear door of the car. We both knew it could only be one person—the President of the Church.

Part of me wanted to do just what Ken was doing—to get as close to the car as I could and shake the Prophet's hand and look into his eyes. But the memory of what I'd felt in the back of that pickup was still too vivid. I couldn't move. I stood by the west gate to Temple Square. Ken waved for me to come over and join him, but I stayed where I was.

Through the open doors of the Tabernacle I could hear the choir rehearsing their songs for the next session of conference. I could hear the excited voices of the crowd that had gathered around the limousine. On the other side of the wall around Temple Square, a police siren blared. But louder than any of the other sounds was the voice in my head: "If you go over there, and he really is a true Prophet of God, he'll look right through you and he'll know you're queer!" What would his reaction be if he could tell? I didn't want to be queer but, I knew that somehow, I was.

The limousine door opened. There he was. From my earliest memory I'd been taught he was a Prophet. Was he? Did he communicate with God in the same way that Moses and Jeremiah and Isaiah had? I wanted to know, but at the same time I was afraid to find out. The spring breeze fluttered his white hair. His smile looked just like the pictures of him I'd seen in Sunday School. He seemed taller than I'd imagined he'd be. Ken stepped forward from the crowd to talk to him. They both looked toward me. I wished I could simply disappear, fade invisibly into the wall. Ken pointed at me. President

McKay looked in my direction and gave me the warmest look I'd ever received from anyone in my whole life. But I couldn't feel any joy in it. I was terrified. He beckoned me to come over to them, and I found myself walking slowly over to where they stood.

The man I had come so far to meet grabbed my right hand in both of his and looked right into my eyes. "It's beautiful weather for conference, isn't it?" he asked me. I just nodded, still unable to speak.

Ken introduced me and told President McKay how we'd driven from California to be at General Conference for the first time in our lives. As the Prophet listened, his clear eyes were framed by what seemed to be a steady and irrepressible glow. I rubbed my eyes to soften the sudden brightness. It must have been the sunlight, I thought to myself.

Back inside the Tabernacle again, Ken told his parents about what had happened. Was he really a Prophet? It had felt good to shake his hand. Could he see through me? Did he know what I really was? What if he weren't a true Prophet?

The Tabernacle was crowded. We'd come early in order to get seats, and we were standing and talking in the balcony so we wouldn't be tired of sitting by the time the meeting was finally ready to start. A few of the General Authorities of the Church were already in their seats. To Mormons, these men were holy men, what Popes and Archbishops are to Roman Catholics. Others were shaking hands with one another and greeting the members seated near the front of the hall. The organ played a soft prelude.

Suddenly, I knew he was in the room. Nothing appeared to be any different than it had been just a minute before, but a powerful feeling of warmth and peace surrounded me and filled me. I turned to Ken. "The Prophet is in the Tabernacle," I told him.

He looked at me strangely, then glanced toward the stand where the First Presidency and Apostles sat. "No, he isn't. Look, his chair is empty."

Personal Dichotomies

I couldn't see him, but still I knew he was in the room. Ken looked all around, and finally leaned over the balcony railing so he could see the doors beneath us. He turned to me in surprise. "You're right! He just came in through the doorway right below us. How did you know?"

My eyes filled with tears. I watched my Prophet make his way slowly toward the front of the Tabernacle. His whole body seemed to radiate light. He was filled with light. I could not stop looking at him. It seemed almost too much to believe. I realized that the glow from his face I'd seen just minutes before as we stood shaking hands outside the Tabernacle must not been have the sunlight, after all. I couldn't hold back the tears of joy and Ken's mother hugged me as I stood there. Then, I felt a voice declare, "Behold, your Prophet." For the first time in my life, God had shown me a sign. I wouldn't speak of this experience until years later in a talk at Brigham Young University when, as a part of a devotional assembly, I shared this experience with my fellow students.

I'd asked and God had given me an answer.

* * * * * * *

God knew how I felt about His Prophets. He knew that after that experience in the Tabernacle in Salt Lake, I'd tried to read every word President McKay spoke or wrote. He knew I'd committed myself, seriously and solemnly, to obey the teachings of this Prophet and of every other Prophet that would follow him in the leadership of the Church.

God had shown me personally that I should follow this man and I had done my best to do that. For me, he was no different than Moses or Elijah or any of the other men of the Bible who walked and talked with God. I became known as a defender of the Prophets. People had told me, after hearing me speak, that the strength of my conviction was enough to make them want to believe simply because I obviously had such a strong belief.

9

God knew that. He knew my heart. He knew how much I wanted to do what was right. But I just didn't know any more what that was. The Prophets said it was wrong for me to want to be close to another man in the way that I had always inwardly and irrepressiby desired to be. Their sermons left no room for any discussion whatsoever on the subject. I'd heard them many times. Homosexuality was a sin, a despicable, degrading, awful sin, one of the "unholy and impure practices" spoken of in the temple.

As I had sustained the Prophets in all they'd taught since I'd received my personal witness of David O. McKay's call, I also defended this position as well. I could not control what I felt, but I could control what I did. I'd vowed to myself that, no matter how strong my desires were for another man, I would never act on those impulses.

And God knew I'd been true to that commitment. But if I was doing what I was supposed to be doing, if I was doing what the Prophets taught, then why did I feel so...so unhappy? So frustrated. Why did I feel that what we'd done to Sergio was so very wrong? My tears seemed to increase.

No comfort came. God who, in this place above all others, should have been close to me, had left me totally alone. He wouldn't hear me. Why? So many times before this Church court we'd held regarding Sergio's situation, I'd received answer to my prayers in the temple. What was wrong this time? Was it Sergio?

I remembered pondering homosexuality as a missionary in Peru many years earlier...

* * * * * * *

Elder Hatch, my missionary companion, knocked half-heartedly on the next door in the small apartment complex where we'd been "tracting" most of the afternoon without much success. Tracting was our method of going door to door in an effort to meet prospective investigators for our Church. We were both very tired.

Personal Dichotomies

"Let's go after this one," he suggested. I agreed. A door opened across the way and a young woman called out to us to come over and talk to her.

"What are you doing here?" she asked as we approached her front step.

"We're missionaries," I answered. "And we have a very important message for you." As she listened, I recited the carefully memorized story of Joseph Smith, the founder of Mormonism, who as a young boy had wanted to know the truth about God and religion. "He read in the Bible," I told her. "'If any of you lack wisdom, let him ask of God,' and then he decided that that's just what he would do."

"Y. . .qué pasó?" She asked. "What happened?"

I told the familiar story. "Joseph went to a grove of trees near his home. He knelt down and began to pray to God, to ask which of all the many churches he should join. As he prayed, he felt overcome by an overpowering darkness; it pushed him to the ground. When he came to himself, he saw two heavenly beings standing above him in the air. One spoke to Joseph and said, pointing to the other, 'This is my beloved son. Hear him.'"

She wanted us to come in and tell her more. We asked if her husband was home. "No, but he'll be here later. Come back and eat with us tonight."

She was pleased when we called her "Hermana Griego." She said she'd like to be our sister. We assured her we'd be back in the evening.

When we returned, Mr. Griego wasn't home, but another man was there. He had an interest in our message. This man was Sister Griego's brother, and he introduced himself to us as Pepe Gomez. He indicated to us that his wife was in the back of the house.

"Why doesn't she come out and join us too?" Elder Hatch asked.

"No," her husband answered, shrugging his shoulders uncomfortably. "You see, she's not able to speak and her noises would be too distracting."

11

We persisted and finally he went to the curtain separating the rooms and called, "Ven, Chica." A thin, pleasant woman ducked nervously into the room and sat down by her husband. Though she was unable to speak, she sat and listened as Elder Hatch and I taught her and her husband and Sister Griego about the gospel.

Through the next two weeks, we continued to teach the two couples. They were eager to learn and listened earnestly as we taught of the apostasy that had followed Christ's crucifixion, and then of the promised restoration that had brought the full sealing blessings of The Holy Priesthood power back to the earth.

One afternoon, as I was speaking on the power the Priesthood has, I felt a gentle pull on the sleeve of my shirt. Chica had come silently up beside me. She put her hands out together in front of her and moved them in a small tentative circle, her eyes all the time watching mine to see if I understood. I shook my head to show my confusion, and she repeated the gesture, this time making a small, definite downward motion with her two hands as if she were laying hands on someone's head.

"She wants to be healed by your Priesthood, Elder Feliz," her husband told me. "She's already told me she knows she'll be healed."

I looked at Elder Hatch. He gave me a small scared half-smile that let me know he'd support me in whatever I decided. But I couldn't tell her no. I'd blessed others, of course, and I'd seen healings, but this was the first time I'd been asked to anoint and lay hands on someone who was totally unable to speak. Would she be healed?

Elder Hatch poured the holy oil to the crown of Chica's head. I then put my hands over his and, after sealing his holy anointing on her head as one from a servant of God, I waited for the Spirit to give me the words. Through me, God then commended her faith, and blessed her that if she had sufficient faith, her affliction would be lifted from her. She was also told that her healing was not for her alone, but in order that this might be a witness of the power of the Priesthood which we had brought with us to bless them.

After the blessing, she thanked me in the only way she could, grasping my hands in hers, and smiling her happiness as she made the small awkward noises that were her only form of communication.

We left to attend to our other appointments. By late afternoon, we'd finished all we'd planned for the day and were returning to our apartment for dinner. As we walked down the main commercial street of the downtown area, I heard someone calling me from down below at the bottom of the hill.

"Elder Feliz! Elder Feliz!" I turned to see who it was. Chica and Pepe were running up the hill and she was shouting my name! They had been scouring the town all afternoon to find me and tell me that right after we'd left their home, her speech had come. We laughed and shouted, cavorting like fools in the street, sharing her joy in her wonderful new found power.

It did not take Chica long to learn that she had much to say to everyone. Sometimes it seemed she was trying to make up for a lifetime of not being able to speak. She talked and talked. And of course we let her.

A few days after the healing, however, as we sat around the Griegos' dinner table, Chica broke into the conversation and said, "I need to clear something up."

"Oh, no, don't listen to her Elders," her sister-in-law warned. She turned to Chica. "You hush now. That's enough of that."

Elder Hatch glanced at me. We both stood at the same time. It seemed best for us to leave, and let the family resolve this problem, whatever it was. But she was not going to let us leave without saying what was on her mind. "El es maricón!" she shouted as we made our way toward the door.

Maricón? Homosexual? Who? She couldn't possibly be talking about me, could she?

Hermana Griego tried to smooth things over. "Don't believe it, Elder," she reassured us. "No es verdad."

13

Gradually we learned what the truth was. Hermano Gomez, our gentle Pepe, was not really Chica's husband at all. They were living together and Chica had just discovered that he was having an affair with a man he'd met at the casino where he worked.

I set up an appointment to meet with Brother Gomez privately. Elder Hatch and I left the house in turmoil. I knew we couldn't baptize him if he was a homosexual. As missionaries, we had been specifically instructed by our area leaders not to teach the gospel to anyone whom we knew to be homosexual. Homosexuals were not included in our call.

At our interview, Pepe begged me to hear his side of the story. He wanted to be baptized. "Sí, Elder Feliz," he admitted, "I am a homosexual. But I am also living with a woman and she has my child. Shouldn't I be baptized so I can raise my boy in the Church?" This man was my brother. I didn't want to be the one to have to make this kind of decision about his future. "I've known it for a long time," he went on. "I started to live with Chica so no one would know. Your Church has so much truth. I thought maybe you'd understand."

I didn't understand. It would be a long time before I'd understand.

* * * * * * *

I glanced toward the sealing room where shortly the young bride and groom and their families would be joining me. I had been entrusted with the sacred sealing power of Elijah, the Keys of Holy Priesthood. Why, then, wouldn't God take these feelings from me? I couldn't imagine how I could pray any more earnestly. Why had God refused to hear me?

My tears became more constant.

A faint but now familiar sound came into me. My pain lifted, separating itself from me, layer by layer. Very slowly, in one of those ways wherein things take place almost imperceptibly, the suffering I was experiencing left. A oneness with

Personal Dichotomies

The Divine filled me, starting at my very core and spreading out until even the tips of my fingers knew the sense of expansion.

God did hear me!

A hushed murmur filled the room—the same sound I had heard many, many times before when upwards of three hundred people had filled this room and joyously greeted each other in happy whispers. The sound of hundreds of whispered voices communicating their joy in being together. I had always been moved by that sound; it was the same sound I was now hearing.

But I was alone! No one was anywhere in sight. I looked up. Three shimmering crystal chandeliers hung above me, representing the three glories of the highest plane of existence. Each prism caught the light and reflected it until the whole room was filled with light. I was myself, but more than myself. I was one with all that is. Love, as warm and protective as something tangible, wrapped itself around me, enfolding me, encircling me, holding me safe in its glow. It surrounded me, held me, lifted me. I saw it all. Love IS Priesthood power. The creative force, the strength that saves us, changes us, exalts us. I was bathed in it. The whispering sound became a rush.

God loved me! The power in the love God had for me surpassed any other power I had ever known, or could even imagine.

The whispering rush became louder and louder. The sound was so loud that I found myself looking toward the north and south doors. It seemed that others might hear it too and come to see what was happening. Then, as suddenly as it had begun, the sound faded. The room was quiet again.

Peace. . .such peace.

The south door opened and a temple ordinance worker walked into the room and started toward me. I dried the tears I'd been unable to hold back, nodded to him, and started for the sealing room where I would perform the sealing.

Out of the Bishop's Closet

Yes, God loved me! The knowledge of it rang through me. Everything in the Church told me that I was evil, that my desires were sinful. But how could that be? How could anyone experience what I'd just experienced and be "bad" or "evil"? It wasn't possible. I knew it. I was worthy of God's love. Somehow, what I'd been taught in the Church about people like me no longer seemed to fit. I didn't understand how it all could make sense. I just knew what I needed to know. I'd come to know I was not evil and God did love me as I was.

The members of the wedding party began to enter the room where I waited. Proud parents. Friends. The young bride and groom, holding hands, nervous, but excited. They looked at me with something a little like awe and I knew they trusted me. There was still so much I didn't understand, but somehow it was all right. I was worthy of their trust. I only needed to trust God the way this young couple trusted me. God loved me.

'Tis the gift to be simple--
'Tis the gift to be free--
'Tis the gift to come down where we ought to be.
And, when we find ourselves in the place that's right,
It will be in the valley of Love and Delight!

When true simplicity is gained,
To bow and to bend, we shant be ashamed.
To turn, turn, will be our delight--
Till by turning, turning, we come out right!

Old Shaker Folk Tune

Chapter 2
Ecclesiastical Contradictions

Laura and I stood on the hardwood floor the contractors had just laid on the concrete foundation. Joseph, Rafael, and Lynne, our children, were with a friend while we tried to decide if we were really going to buy this home in Sandy, Utah. Through the new windows, I could see six or seven foundations with homes in various stages of construction. The places where other houses would be built were marked only by gaping holes in the sandy ground.

We walked outside. Far away to the west, the copper mine was a scar against the Oquirrh mountains, and to the east, the Wasatch mountains caught the last reflected glow of the reddish-orange sunset. It was going to be a good neighborhood. We could feel it. Hand in hand, we walked around the lot together. I looked at the unfinished building, and tried to imagine it a home, our home. But the reasons we couldn't buy it seemed too overwhelming. Where would we get a down payment? Closing costs. Taxes. Insurance. Could we qualify? We'd never owned a home before. My salary at Church headquarters was insufficient.

Back inside the house again, we wandered through the empty rooms, and then finally sat down on the floor of what would become the living room. I finally said to Laura, "Well? Do you want to go for it?"

"Do you?"

"I asked you first."

19

"You're the cutie," she answered, teasing me for not wanting to say what I thought until she did.

"Well, you're cuti-er!"

As usual, that got to her. She laughed. "If you feel good about it, then that's what we should do." She had always been willing to support me in my decisions about our family. This would be no different.

I stood and looked through the wood frame to the northwest. The sunset had almost faded. A strange sensation filled me. A feeling that somehow I knew all the people that would move into the unfinished houses up and down this street. And not only that I knew them, but that I...that we even somehow belonged there.

Laura sensed my sudden change in mood. "What, Tony?"

"Nothing." But my reassurance sounded hollow even to me. "Let's go back to the car."

I started the car. Again I felt it. The strongest sense that I wanted to put my arms around this whole area and all the people in it and protect them and hold them and lift them. That even though I didn't know their names, I knew them, their needs, their fears, their deepest pain. An almost overwhelming sense of responsibility flooded through me. I couldn't move to shift the car into gear. "Hey," Laura said gently, "you know we're going to have to talk about this sometime. Why don't you just tell me now?"

"If we move into this 'ward,'" I began slowly, "they're going to make me...they're going to make me the Bishop." I took her hand in mine. "Do you think you're ready to be the Bishop's wife?" A ward is the Mormon equivalent of a Catholic parish; it is the local congregation of the Church.

We were living in a ward near the Capitol in Salt Lake City at the time. Being a Bishop was the farthest thought from my mind. I taught the young adult gospel doctrine class and I loved it. The members of the class were motivated and well-educated and the course of study was Church history, always one of my favorite topics. Our Bishop was a good man and I respected him. Five months ago, he had given me an assignment which had now become one of the major reasons Laura and I were considering moving from Salt Lake City to Sandy...

* * * * * * *

I could tell as soon as I walked into the Bishop's office that he had something important to ask me. He asked briefly about my family. A few pleasantries about the class I was teaching followed. Then he asked unexpectedly, "What do you know about Jim Bastewort?"

I was silent.

What did I know about him? Jim was a tall, good-looking man in our Ward. I knew my eyes were always diverted to him whenever he walked into a room. My mouth grew dry. Certainly I had never let any of these feelings show, had I? I tried to swallow. Bishops were supposed to have the gift of discernment. Did my Bishop discern my inner attractions?

"Do you know who I mean?" the Bishop persisted.

"Yes, I know him. He's the one who's been dating all the girls in my class." I waited nervously for his response.

"Yes, that's the one I mean, Tony. I have something very special for you to do for the Church and for Jim."

"Of course, Bishop." My answer was quick and automatic. "What do you need me to do?" Like every good Mormon, I had covenanted in the Temple of God to consecrate my all to the Church. I was ready to do whatever he asked.

"Good. I knew I could count on you. You'll be working closely with me and with the office of Elder Mark E. Peterson of The Council of The Twelve."

Elder Peterson? I felt a tremor of apprehension. What kind of assignment would involve one of The Twelve Apostles?

Jim had been suspected of being heavily involved with a polygamist group and it appeared he was trying to convert some of the young women of our Ward. My assignment was to befriend him, gain his confidence, and report back to Elder

21

Peterson's office. The Church authorities wanted to know the names of the people he met with, where they met, the license numbers of their vehicles, and anything else I could find out. Laura was not to know anything about it, except as cleared through the Bishop. I agreed to do what I could to help. Over the next three months I began to live two separate lives: one with Jim and his friends and another with everyone else. As we met privately in small discussion groups to discuss the gospel and polygamy, I discovered there were many, many others in the valley who also believed in the "principle" and were trying seriously and sincerely to live it to the fullest.

We met in secret; polygamy is against the law. Jim was trying to convert the girls in our class. He wanted to marry as many of them as would have him. I attended the meetings and dutifully reported back to the Bishop. I wasn't sure what Elder Peterson's office was going to do with this information, but I trusted my leaders. It's what I'd been taught to do.

One evening a group of us gathered at the home of a former seminary instructor who had been excommunicated from the Mormon Church. Jared wanted to help me see that the Priesthood and the institutional Church were two totally separate and distinct bodies. "Don't you remember that the Priesthood was here months before the Church even got organized?" he pointed out. "When was the Priesthood given to Joseph Smith and Oliver Cowdery?"

"May 15, 1829," I answered. "When they baptized each other."

"And when did they ordain each other?"

"Right after their baptisms."

"When was the Church organized?"

"April 6, 1830."

"Right." He paused, waiting to see if my mind would reach the logical conclusion that followed.

I strained at it. In my mind, the Church and the Priesthood had always been inseparably connected. How could one use Priesthood without a church? I couldn't imagine one existing without the other.

"Don't you see," he insisted, "that the Priesthood functioned for almost a year without a church? Just as it can now. Priesthood doesn't need an institution."

Suddenly the door burst open. One of Jared's wives rushed into the room, carrying his smallest son in her arms. The child whimpered in pain and his left hand hung limp and awkward as he held it motionless against his small body. He'd fallen from the bed of a truck outside their home, and had apparently tried to use his hand to break his fall. Even my untrained eye could see how unnaturally the bone pushed at the skin of his wrist.

Without consulting among themselves, all the men in the room except me immediately gathered around the child and placed their hands on him. Calling upon the power of the Priesthood they all held, Jared blessed his son that he would be made whole. The child was still as his father spoke, holding his injured arm carefully in his lap, palm down. Suddenly, as I watched, his wrist seemed to jerk out and then back in, almost as if an unseen hand had touched the broken bone, skillfully setting it back into its proper place. Surprised, the boy flinched for an instant as his arm moved, then cautiously began to flex his hand back and forth. Jared set him on the floor and he ran back to his mother to be picked up, both hands outstretched.

The next day, I went to the Bishop and told him what I'd seen. "Tony," he admonished me, "it's essential that you not tell anyone about what you've been doing for me. It's especially important that you not tell anyone about this healing." He paused, as if wondering if he could really say what he wanted to, then finally continued, "Tony, I think it might be a good idea for you and Laura to consider moving out of the Ward."

* * * * * * *

Our first Sunday in the Sandy 82nd Ward was an eye-opener for both Laura and me. The chapel of the small church building was filled to capacity; the folding doors dividing the

23

cultural hall from the chapel were open and that room was half full as well. Most of the people there were infants in their parents' arms. As more people came into the chapel, the sound of crying babies grew to an almost incessant din.

We found a place and sat down. I watched the families filtering in as they found seats. As I looked and saw, I sensed something a little disconcerting. I turned to Laura. "Are you sure we made the right decision?" I whispered.

"Why?"

"Look around you." She looked around the large congregation and saw immediately what I meant. My children and I were the only non Anglo-Saxons present. "When they make me Bishop," I said in a low voice so only she could hear me, "a lot of people here aren't going to like it one bit."

She shrugged and shook her head and reached to straighten Rafael's tie. She was right. There was no backing out now. We'd bought the house, watched the conclusion of the construction, and moved in. And if I was meant to be Bishop, then I was meant to be Bishop.

Perhaps we should have been used to prejudice. We'd certainly seen enough of it. I wasn't though. It was one of those things that always caught me totally off guard, no matter how I tried to prepare myself. Our experiences as the object of ethnic bigotry began when we first decided to get married. It was 1967. I was a junior at Brigham Young University...

* * * * * * *

My Bishop had counseled me to get married. "All those tendencies will go away when you get married, Tony. It is only a phase." I had confessed my inward desires as part of my religious duty. I thought that this would be last time I would ever tell anyone.

Elder Marion G. Romney was visiting Brigham Young University to speak at a devotional assembly. Laura and I, who were seriously considering marriage, determined that while he was there, we would ask him for his counsel. At that time

Ecclesiastical Contradictions

Mormon leaders taught openly that "mixed marriages" should be avoided, and that all young people should seek out partners of their own ethnic and racial background. This was years and many social changes before Blacks began to be included in the Priesthood.

Laura and I were both faithful, committed members of the Church and we wanted to follow the counsel of our Church leaders. We both felt it was the right thing for us to marry, but still we wanted some reassurance. As we approached President Romney, he could see we were hand in hand. We introduced ourselves by name, but before I had a chance to say anything else, he said, "Yes, of course, I'll marry you. Just get with my secretary and set up an appointment." We hadn't even had a chance to mention marriage!

I looked at Laura in confusion. She winked at me. Brother Romney was ready to turn to someone else in the waiting crowd. "No," I blurted out. "What we really wanted to ask you about was the question of mixed marriages."

"Well, go ahead and set up two appointments, then," he said quickly. "One for the visit and another for the temple. But don't worry. I'll marry you two."

That night Laura called her parents to tell them she was engaged to be married in the Salt Lake Temple by one of the Twelve Apostles. But apparently all they could hear was my surname. Laura held the receiver away from her ear, and I could hear her father's angry exclamations. "Feliz? You mean he's a Mexican? You're going to marry a Mexican?"

She put the phone back to her ear. For a long time she said nothing. Finally, she hung up the telephone and began to cry.

"What?" I asked in bewilderment, taking her into my arms and brushing her tears away with awkward fingers.

"He said he's going to come after you with a gun," she said when she was finally able to speak.

"What?" How could they hate me so much just because I had a Spanish surname? They were good Mormon people. Laura's father was from one of the old pioneer families that had first settled the cities of northern Utah. Her mother was a product of two plural marriages and had been born in the colonies the early polygamists had established in Mexico to escape the persecution of the United States government. Why would they have such strong negative feelings against me just because my name was Feliz?

Laura tried to explain. Apparently there was a long history of prejudice in her family on both sides because of some unfortunate experiences in the Mexican colonies as well as in Las Vegas, Nevada, where they'd later lived. She didn't elaborate. It should have been a time of joy for us. We'd wanted to share that joy.

Later, I asked Rodney Turner, who was then my Bishop, about prejudice in the Church. Bishop Turner was a professor of religion on campus whom we respected. He'd help to calm us down. "Tony," he counseled, "the gospel of Christ is true. It's true in spite of the people who profess to believe it. There's always going to be prejudice in the Church and you're going to feel the impact of that prejudice a lot more than most others do. Just remember that the gospel is true in spite of the people who profess to believe it."

* * * * * * *

It was time for the meeting to start. What was it going to be like to be Bishop here? I had a feeling that I was going to find out what Bishop Turner had been talking about.

Three weeks after Laura and I had moved into our new home, I sat in the Stake President's office for an 8:00 p.m. interview. Much like a Catholic diocese is presided over by a Catholic Bishop, a group of wards in the Mormon Church are organized into a stake which is presided over by a Stake Presidency of three men. All three members of my Stake Presidency were there, warmly getting to know me as the interview progressed. I'd told Laura before I left home that tonight would be the night that they'd do their best to determine that I was to be the new Bishop of our Ward. Within two weeks a subsequent interview produced the official call from the Stake Presidency. The Presiding Bishopric and the Twelve Apostles had approved their recommendation to make me the first Bishop of the anticipated new ward.

Days after Laura and I both accepted the call, six hundred hands were raised to manifest the agreement of our fellow Church members to my ordination and call as their new Bishop. A Bishop in the Mormon Church serves with the assistance of two councilors and my first sense of Divine direction in this ministry was when I received direction on who my two counselors were to be. The three of us became very close in the Priesthood ministry of serving the spiritual needs of our Ward members.

The area continued to grow rapidly. As more new homes were completed, other families and young couples moved into the community. Only a few months later, a new stake was formed: the Wasatch East Sandy South Stake of Zion. The creation of our new stake required the supervision of an Apostle. Elder LeGrand Richards supervised the proceedings. As part of his search for the new president of the Stake, he interviewed each Bishop. I personally had no doubts about who the next Stake President would be. He was the Bishop of the Ward with which we shared our building.

He was with Elder Richards when I was called in for a second interview with the visiting Apostle from Church headquarters.

"Bishop Feliz," Elder Richards began, "I'd like you to meet your new Stake President."

"Congratulations, President." I extended my hand to shake his. He hesitated momentarily, then took my hand and gave it a cursory shake.

"Do you feel you can support your new president fully in his calling?" Elder Richards asked.

Actually, Bishop Farnsworth and I had had a few minor disagreements regarding our combined use of the physical facilities, and I'd been frustrated by his stubborn refusal to try to see things from our perspective. But that was immaterial now. He'd been called to preside over me. From the day I'd received the manifestation regarding David O. McKay, I'd always sustained my Priesthood leaders totally. This would be no different.

I shared this conviction with the two of them. "I've always supported my Priesthood leaders and I will continue to do so." I tried to look the soon-to-be president in the eye as I said this, but he would not meet my gaze. He was looking at Elder Richards as if he were waiting for him to say something further. But Elder Richards didn't speak.

Finally, Bishop Farnsworth nudged him and said, "Didn't you...didn't you want to inquire about that other subject?" He glanced at me as he said it. I realized they'd been talking about me before I'd come in.

The Apostle leaned toward me. He looked me directly in the eyes, "Bishop," he asked, "are you homosexual?"

Of everything he might have asked, this was absolutely the last question I'd expected. I looked from the Apostle to Bishop Farnsworth in disbelief. I was in shock.

Yes, I'd felt strong desires for intimacies with other men. Of course I had; I couldn't deny that. But I'd never acted on those desires. Never! I'd walked away from the opportunities that had presented themselves. I'd turned away from temptation. And for what? To be accused of exactly what I had fought so hard to resist? I was incensed with anger. I had hoped that if I resisted these tendencies long enough they would go away, that maybe they were just some kind of test for me. And now, an inescapable injustice forced me to look at it, painful though it was.

"No." I answered flatly. "Of course not. What have I been accused of?" I was not yet able to admit to myself that I was gay. How could I admit it to anyone else? That step was beyond my emotional abilities at that time.

Neither one of them answered. I looked at Bishop Farnsworth. He looked at the floor. I had no doubt but that he was my accuser.

Ecclesiastical Contradictions

Finally, Elder Richards turned to my new Stake President. "President," he said, "I believe this man should continue with his calling for the rest of his tenure. There is no sin here."

Turning to me he added, "Sorry, Bishop, but we felt the need to ask you about this. Keep up the good work in your Ward."

There were no apologies from President Farnsworth. After an awkward pause, I thanked them for their vote of confidence in me and reexpressed my commitment to the Church and to the Kingdom of God. They thanked me for coming, and asked me to invite the next Bishop in as I left.

Alone outside the interviewing room, I leaned against the brick wall of the corridor. How could he do it? This man who was about to be made my file Priesthood leader knew nothing of me—of my dedication and persistence, of the honest effort I'd made to be a righteous man worthy of the blessings of a just God. He hadn't seen the tenacity with which I held to my covenants. He saw only what he wanted to see. How could he possibly take it upon himself to accuse me of something that I hadn't really even considered doing since my adolecence?

It was going to be difficult to support him, but I would do my best. He was now my President.

A year passed.

One morning at a meeting in the Church Office Building where I worked in the Welfare Services Department, a member of our department brought up a major problem that was being observed more and more frequently in the stakes of the Church.

"Welfare farms are established for one purpose," he told us, "and for one purpose only. These projects have been set up throughout the Church so that the poor can be provided for. These farms give the members the opportunity to work together so that those less fortunate than they can be taken care of."

"But we have a problem," he continued. "Too many Stake Presidents are authorizing the use of the Church welfare farms in their control for purposes other than this. They've lost the vision of what is possible as saints throughout the world join in working together to take care of each other."

When he finished, Victor L. Brown, the Presiding Bishop of the Church, stood, and added his impassioned plea that all of us do what we could to help solve this problem and return things to the way the Lord intended them to be.

"If you personally are aware of any violations of this nature," he asked, "please see that the appropriate members of your departments are notified as promptly as possible. We want to rectify any incorrect uses of the welfare properties. We want to return them to their right and proper function in caring for the Lord's poor. We want to be counted among the Lord's disciples, not among the wicked 'being in torment'." He had quoted from the *Doctrine and Covenants*. The *Doctrine and Covenants* is a book which Mormons accept as scripture.

I faced an uncomfortable dilemma.

Only weeks before, President Farnsworth had proposed to our Stake Council of Bishops that our Stake welfare farm be used as a baseball field.

When I returned home from work the night of the meeting, I retired to my study. I needed to be alone. I picked up my old *Doctrine and Covenants*. I began to read what the scripture said about the care of the poor and needy. The Lord's word was clear. Over and over again we were admonished to impart of our substance to care for the poor, to remember the afflicted among us, and share with them, "as becometh saints." The failure to do so was, in the eyes of God, obviously a serious offense.

And yet, I felt a strong need to support my Stake President as I had promised I would when he was called. I determined at last that it was best for me to remain silent on the whole matter. I didn't see what else I could do.

Ecclesiastical Contradictions

I continued to turn the pages of my scriptures. In section 104 of the *Doctrine and Covenants*, verse 18 hit me with power:

Therefore, If any man shall take of the abundance which I have made, and impart not his portion, according to the law of my gospel, unto the poor and the needy, he shall, with the wicked, lift up his eyes in hell, being in torment.

They were the same words the Presiding Bishop had used. I realized I could not remain silent. But before going to my superiors in the Welfare Services Department, I would go to President Farnsworth and share my quandary with him. I'd put it squarely in his lap, and give him the opportunity to make any changes he thought necessary.

In the next council meeting of the Bishops of our Stake, President Farnsworth announced that instead of purchasing the land adjacent to the new stake center for use as recreational property for the Stake, he was encouraging us to approve the purchase of property at the far southern boundary of the Stake.

As we discussed his proposal, there seemed to be two major problems with it. First, most of us could see no reason to choose land that was miles away from the stake center when there was land right next to it for sale. And, second, the alternate property proposed for purchase by the Stake President just happened to be deeded in his father's name.

As we began to leave the meeting, President Farnsworth made one last announcement. "We have to hurry on this decision, Bishops," he said. "The Church Offices staff is on our backs to stop using the Church welfare farm for our youth sports program, so we need to get this resolved as quickly as we can."

It's customary for Bishops to go back to the Priesthood members in their respective wards in order to propose and seek a sustaining vote on any proposals that involve financial commitments from them as individual contributors. I knew as I left the meeting that I simply could not, in good conscience, ask the brethren of my Ward to support a proposal like the one President Farnsworth had just made. A proposal that was obviously self-serving and not in the best interest of the Stake members living in our wards close to the stake center.

I decided that when I met with President Farnsworth to share my concerns about the use of the welfare farm, I would discuss this issue with him as well. I would share my feelings with him. Perhaps there were some other aspects of the situation I wasn't fully aware of. If I went to him and expressed my concerns openly and honestly, he, as my Priesthood leader, would surely be able to help me find a way to sustain his proposal.

The Stake President didn't stand as I entered his office for our interview two nights later. With an impatient gesture, he motioned me to the chair across from his desk. When I was seated, he finally spoke.

"Bishop Feliz, I'm extremely disappointed by your recent behavior," he began.

I had no idea what he was talking about. I told him as much.

He gave a snort of disgust. "I'm sure you don't." His voice was filled with derision and sarcasm. I shifted uncomfortably on the chair, as if I could physically move out of the range of his anger. "Don't you think I know who turned us in to the Church's Welfare Department authorities? Didn't it occur to you I'd have a pretty good idea of who would pull a stunt like that?"

"But..." I tried to say I hadn't done that, that I had come to talk with him before anything else. He didn't give me a chance to speak.

"You thought you could just go over my head, didn't you? I should have known you'd do anything you could to make me look bad!" He was almost shouting at me, then dropped his voice and muttered, seemingly to himself, "Faggot Bishops! What should I expect, working with queers?"

I'd come to talk to him before I said anything to the people in my department about using the welfare farm for the kids to play softball on. I'd wanted to hear his side of the issue of buying his father's property for the Stake. I'd wanted to be true to my commitment to sustain him as my President.

"Look, Bishop," he said, pronouncing the word "Bishop" as if it were the most degrading of epithets, "I have only one thing to say to you. If you don't recommend this proposal to your Priesthood brethren, I'll have your Church membership for disobedience. And don't think I won't. I know what you are."

Driving down the dark country road back to my home, I couldn't hold the tears back. He was right. I'd tried and tried to push my real feelings down so deep inside me that no one would ever know who I really was. But it didn't make any difference. It never would make any difference what I did.

I was faithful to Laura. I loved her. I wouldn't hurt her. I'd leave her, if I had to, before I'd do anything to hurt her. The futility of it all seemed too much to bear. I pulled into my driveway and sat alone in the dark car for a long time, unable to face my family or my responsibilities—or myself. I knew I hadn't fooled anyone, even President Farnsworth could see I was homosexual. I was the only one who couldn't see it.

My tears were bitter.

Early the next Sunday morning, before the meeting at which I'd have to present President Farnsworth's proposal, I met with my two counselors. I loved Rick and Steve, and respected them both for their integrity and their commitment to the gospel. I shared with them my feelings about the proposal and asked for their advice as to how to proceed.

Rick could see immediately the position I was in. He could see that I wanted to support my Stake President, but that I also had to be true to myself. "I think you should have someone else make the proposal," he suggested. "That way, your own vote won't have to be made publicly."

Steve agreed. "You can't do it," he warned. "There's no way you'd be able to keep your true feelings from showing." We knelt and put our arms around each other and prayed that God would direct what happened. I was so grateful for my counselors.

As I stood before the business session of the Priesthood meeting a few minutes later and began to announce the proposal, a member of our Stake High Council walked in through the rear door of the chapel and took his seat in the back. I stopped what I was saying and asked him to come to the front and join me on the stand.

"The business at hand is a proposal from the Stake President," I said, "and it is right and fitting that you represent him here in case there are any questions." The brother came up and took a seat beside me. With him here, I knew I would have to handle the business myself. I announced the proposal to purchase the land recommended by President Farnsworth, and then asked, "Is there any discussion on this matter?"

An elder stood up in the back of the chapel. "Who owns that land, Bishop?"

"I'm not sure," I lied. "Perhaps this member of our High Council can help us." The brother claimed he didn't know either.

Another elder raised his hand to speak. "I understand that that land belongs to the Stake President himself."

A member of the Stake who was not a member of our Ward stood up. "It is important for all of you to know that the land in question isn't owned by President Farnsworth. It's deeded in the name of his father. It's not the President's personal property."

A heated discussion followed. Strong opinions were expressed—both in favor of the proposal and against it. Finally, I was able to call for a vote.

"It is proposed..." I began. One of the men who had been most vocal interrupted me before I could go any further.

"Bishop, before the vote, would you tell us how you feel about this proposal?"

My mind went blank.

Later, my counselors reported to me that I said the following: "I sustain my Priesthood leader. All in favor of the proposal of the Stake President may manifest it by the usual sign." They told me I raised my own right hand, signifying my public sustaining vote, and then continued, "All those opposed may manifest it in the same manner."

Mormon business meetings usually are rather uneventful in that members of the Church are conditioned to simply agree and follow with their leaders on any proposal. The record showed, however, that nearly two thirds of the brethren present voted against this proposal. It was something I had never seen happen before.

Following our vote, the brother from the Stake High Council came up to the pulpit. "Brethren," he said, "I should advise you that this vote today is moot—a mere formality. The property was purchased in the name of the Stake last week."

A murmur of discontent spread through the assembled group. Like me, they simply could not believe that the principle of common consent, touted as one of the foundation doctrines of Latter-day Saint theology, could be so blatantly disregarded.

My safe, secure, predictable world heaved around me. I tried to remind myself of what Rodney Turner had taught me so long before, that the gospel was true in spite of the people. I didn't expect the leaders to be perfect. I accepted them as men, men that had problems and weaknesses just as I did. But, I somehow expected more than this.

None of it made sense any more: prejudice and greed and fear on one side; on the other, Jared, an apostate, with his son safe and whole in his arms. The painful clamor of President Farnsworth's threats and accusations. The whispered rushing hush of heavenly hosts, immediate and close, as I sat alone in the temple. A lifetime of commitment and devotion. For this? I'd been willing to give everything I had to the Church. I simply did not know where to turn.

The institution that had embodied my religious faith was now showing itself as incapable of holding the completeness of my commitment.

Prest. Smith rose...Said the Lord had declared by the prophet that the people should each one stand for himself and depend on no man or men...that righteous persons could only deliver their own souls--applied it to the present state of the church of Latter Day Saints--Said if the people departed from the Lord, they must fall--that they were depending on the prophet hence darkened in their minds from neglect of themselves...

Nauvoo Relief Society Minutes
26 May 1842

Chapter 3
Prophets, Seers,
and Revelators

Dr. James O. Mason, director of the Developing Welfare Services Department and my immediate supervisor, called me into his office.

He was a direct man and did not waste any time getting to the point of the visit. "Tony," he asked, "what do you know about the Law of Consecration and Stewardship?"

"Well, I studied quite a bit of Church history at BYU," I said. "And that's a subject I've made a personal avocation of by daily study of the *Doctrine and Covenants*."

And for some reason, this particular aspect of Church history had always fascinated me. Whenever I'd turned to the scriptures or to the history of the Church, it was the passages dealing with the establishment of Zion that I found myself returning to again and again. If it really were possible to create a Zion people, a society like the one Enoch had, a people ready for the second coming of Jesus Christ, then surely the key to making that happen was to be found in a fuller understanding of the true meaning of the word "consecrate."

Doctor Mason listened and nodded as I shared my feelings with him, almost as if he'd known already how I felt. "Good. I want you to continue your study," he told me. "Only now you'll have access to all the materials in the Church Historical Department. If possible, we want you to gather in one location all that's been taught relative to these principles by all the Presidents of the Church."

"Can you tell me why you want this?"

"As you well know, Tony," he said, "the Church is no longer a Utah church or even an American church. It's an international church. Missionaries are teaching the gospel to people who live in cultures totally different from those we're familiar with—people living under completely different economic systems, different forms of government. By studying what our leaders taught in the past on consecration and stewardship, and by reviewing what was done as the earlier saints endeavored to implement these principles, we hope we can develop a series of basic principles that can be applied in the development of Church Welfare Services worldwide—principles that go beyond any limitation of any single or particular cultural orientation."

"We take our commitment to care for the poor seriously. We want to encourage self-sufficiency and teach people to manage their resources wisely and effectively, but at the same time, we feel a real responsibility to help those who are less fortunate than we are. As Jesus said, 'to feed his sheep.' We need to be sure that the money we spend to care for the poor in third and fourth-world nations is used in the best way possible, in the way that will do the most good for the most people."

I still did not quite see the connection.

"I think you will as you study and continue your research on this," he said. "I want you to prepare a presentation to give for the First Presidency." The First Presidency consists of the Prophet and his two Counselors. It is the highest authoritative body of the Mormon Church.

Dr. Mason smiled. Thinking about President Spencer W. Kimball somehow lifted him. "You know, once when President Kimball and I were discussing this subject, he said to me something I've never forgotten. He said, 'I would rather close down all the temples throughout the world than fail in our responsibility to care for the poor.'"

Close the temples? Is that possible? Had the President of our Church even considered such a drastic act?

"But there's a better way than that. And we need your help in determining what it is. When you think you've found it, let me know."

I left his office, but couldn't go back to my own. I walked out into the fall sunshine. The grounds of the Church Office Building were bright with flowers and fountains. The season's first yellow leaves were light in the air, twisting in the autumn breeze. Occasionally in our lives, there are moments when we know with an absolute certainty that what we are about is exactly what we need to be about, times when we know that where we are and what we're doing is totally and completely right. This was one of those times. The fountains splashed their melody to the wind. The marigolds and asters shone as if they were the source of their own light. There was a key hidden in the Church archives, and all we knew was that it was there. We weren't even sure what the door was that it would unlock. And I was the one who'd been asked to find it. The sense of my own destiny filled me and spread out from me, radiating like an uncontainable force.

The next few months were some of the most stimulating of my entire career as an employee of the Mormon Church. Here I was, an insignificant bureaucratic employee of the Church, given an almost "carte blanche" access to documents of extremely sensitive historical significance. I spent hours looking at microfilmed documents and, where necessary, at the documents themselves in secure areas of the archives.

My preliminary research confirmed what I already knew from my study of the *Doctrine and Covenants* and Church history—unless we were "equal in earthly things," we could not be "equal in heavenly things." The saints had tried many times to establish "united orders" and had succeeded for varying lengths of time. They'd called them by various names: the Order of Enoch, the Order of All Things in Common, the Economic Order of the Son of God, the Order of Unity. And in the end, they had all failed.

The records did not always make the reasons clear. It seemed too easy to say that people were simply selfish. Heber

39

C. Kimball compared the orders to thriving plants that "blossomed forth for a season, and then under the scorching sun of traditional error...withered and died."

I turned to the minutes of meetings held by the First Presidencies of the Church, meetings of the Twelve Apostles, and of the Presiding Bishoprics. I read the journals kept by Wilford Woodruff and other early leaders of the Church. These were the men who had framed the theological foundations of Mormonism and I was privileged to share their deepest and most personal thoughts.

From the roots of the old united orders of the late 1800's, I saw the projects develop that were the predecessors of the welfare farms, canneries and production plants the Church would later own and operate. These enterprises would give members of the Church opportunities to donate their time and labor in the production of food and other necessities that could later be distributed to those in need.

I began to catch a glimpse not only of how these principles might apply to the poor in the developing nations of the world, but also of how they were at the very center of the gospel of Jesus Christ. I began to organize what I'd discovered for my presentation before the First Presidency of the Church.

On the day scheduled for our meeting, Doctor Mason and Victor L. Brown, the Presiding Bishop of the Church, invited me into the large conference room where the First Presidency was waiting. It was an elegant room with richly wood-paneled walls and sumptuous furnishings.

Bishop Brown introduced me to President Spencer W. Kimball. The Prophet clasped both of his hands around my right hand. "It's good to know you," he said. "I'm looking forward to your presentation today."

I suddenly felt quite inadequate. For over six months, I'd studied and read and prayed, and only a few moments before as I walked into the room, I'd felt very well prepared. God had guided me in my research. I knew that. But this man was a Prophet. He held *all* the Keys of Holy Priesthood. He had the ability to communicate with God in a way that was far more direct and immediate than most of us could even imagine. What could I possibly teach him?

"Brother Feliz is a Bishop in the Church, President," the Presiding Bishop continued.

President Kimball glanced at his two counselors, seated on either side of him—President Marion Romney, who had married Laura and me in the Salt Lake Temple years earlier, on one side, and on the other, President N. Eldon Tanner. He looked back at me and smiled warmly to put me at ease. "It's appropriate, isn't it," he said, "for a Bishop to teach us about consecration and stewardship?" Still, I suddenly didn't feel I could teach them a thing.

As I shared a quotation from Heber J. Grant, the seventh President of the Church, to begin my presentation, President Romney interrupted me, "Oh, yes, I remember that meeting. President Grant felt very strongly about this issue." These men had lived the history that I could only study.

There had been some good programs in the early days of what was called the "Church Security Program." This system had eventually developed into the Church Welfare Program. I shared as many of them as I could. The Mormon Church that received national recognition from the Federal Government for this program during the Great Depression. These men had initiated it. I tried to retain my composure.

President Tanner remembered one undertaking especially well. "That little enterprise was a communal effort that surprised everyone," he said when I mentioned one early experiment in cooperative living. "It was one of the most successful cooperative efforts of those depression years that I can recall."

My goal was to show—or remind—these men whom I revered as the Prophets of God, that there were some programs and types of projects that, while no longer applicable to the modern economic society of the United States, could very well apply in third and fourth-world nations—

programs for economies that are similar to what this country, and especially Utah, had experienced during the econnomic depression of the 1930's.

I turned to my charts and began to unfold my dream. "We start with fifty families," I explained. "A community of about 300 people. We provide land for them to grow the food and raise the animals they need, and set them up in a small income-producing industry appropriate to their locale." I pointed to the statistics based on similar programs in the United States. "Within three to five years, the community will have become totally self-sufficient and will probably even be in a position to aid in starting up a neighboring community that can then begin producing something else both groups need."

"Who would own the land?" Bishop Brown asked.

"The Church in Peru. That way we satisfy all the requirements of the local governments."

The others were silent.

"These people are living in poverty. How can we teach them to know God when their children are dying of malnutrition? They're hard-working, dedicated Latter-day Saints. For the price of paying one needy family's monthly rent in Utah, we can start the kind of business that will provide for an entire Peruvian family for a year. Because of their need, these people are ready to live the gospel in a way Utah Mormons aren't. They know they have to share, to work together, that the only way that any of them can succeed is if all of them succeed together. It will only take the smallest amount of help from us to get it started."

I could see it all so clearly. It was what Joseph Smith had envisioned for the saints of his day. Out of small things great things surely could come. Selflessness, cooperation, the willingness to consecrate: these were the foundation stones on which Zion would be built—the utopian society that would be ready for the return of the Lord.

When I'd finished, President Kimball turned to President Tanner. "Do you have any counsel?" he asked.

"My experience is that this kind of program would work in the kinds of situations we're looking at here," President Tanner offered.

"Can we do it?"

"Of course we can," President Tanner said. "There wouldn't be any financial limitations on such a program if we limited it to third and fourth-world nations."

President Romney winked at me as President Tanner shared his observation with President Kimball. "President," he said with enthusiasm, "This is the kind of thing I've been waiting to get on with for over forty years!"

For a moment President Kimball didn't speak. Finally, breaking the awkwardness that was rising in the air, he said, "Brethren, we can't do this yet; the timing is not right." He turned to me. "Bishop, please go and work on this concept again and return with a complete recommendation for our consideration." As he said this, I was filled with a sense of peace.

Yes, I suddenly somehow knew within myself that there was something very important that was missing from my presentation that day. I did not yet know what it was, but with that charge from God's Prophet ringing in my ears, I was sure that I'd find out what it was.

He gave me a firm smile and a small wave of his hand. That was the "high sign," and Bishop Brown whispered to me, "You can leave now. Thank you, Tony."

As I began to gather the equipment and materials I'd brought with me, I overheard Bishop Brown ask about a several-million-dollar request for a grant from the Church for medical research at the University of Utah.

"Oh, of course," the Prophet answered immediately. "That's a program we mustn't hold up any longer."

I wasn't aware of all the details, but I'd heard enough to know one thing: when the program I was recommending was fully completed and ready to be implemented, the finances would be available.

I returned to my office, but somehow the paper-work accumulated on my desk could not hold my attention. The memory of President Kimball's grasp, his voice, his eyes, separated me from the things that usually seemed so important. He'd paid such close attention to what I'd said. I went to the window and looked down at the snow-flurried March afternoon.

He was a Prophet. He opened himself to the Divine and taught us what he learned from that Source. What made him a true prophet? He believed what he taught. There was an urgency in what he said. Was that what false prophets were? Those who taught as messages from God things that they *themselves* did not believe? Were "false" prophets false only because they were "unethical"?

I had just experienced being in the presence of a man who, in his decision, had demonstrated that he was an ethical prophet, a true one. He was a true prophet, an "ethical" prophet. He had taught what he personally received from the Divine Source, not merely what others claimed to have received from that Source. In his presence, I'd also felt his love for me, his personal concern.

But something kept nagging at me, tugging at the back of my mind. What was it? The snow had stopped and the sky was clearing. I watched the clouds dissolve and separate. Then, it came to me. I knew what it was that was bothering me...

It was his book. *The Miracle of Forgiveness*. How could I have forgotten? His written words had burned themselves into my memory when I'd read them. How could I have forgotten chapter six? I had read it over and over again years earlier: *"Let it therefore be clearly stated that the seriousness of the sin of homosexuality is equal to or greater than that of fornication or adultery."* I remembered the words he'd used to describe it: *"ugly...repugnant...unnatural...degenerate."*

I couldn't deny my personal conviction that Spencer Kimball was a true prophet. Being in his presence, it was impossible not to know it. But, if he were, why did he teach what he did about homosexuality? Had God revealed that to him? I had to know.

Revelation? What was it anyway? We claimed it was central to our religion, that the one thing that set Mormonism apart from all the other churches was the fact that this church was led by prophets who received direct communication from God. But how did it work? The Lord had said, *"My thoughts are not your thoughts, neither are your ways my ways."* But if they weren't, if they couldn't be, then how was it even possible for infinite, eternal verities to be put into words we could understand?

No, that wasn't it. We do put them into words. That's what all the prophets since the world began had been trying to do, over and over. Trying to capture their visions, their insights, the truth they knew, and to express them in a way that others could comprehend. The question was: Is eternal, infinite truth changed by putting it into limited, mortal, human language?

A phrase came into my mind—in the temple, my arm raised up heavenward—it was this phrase that always reverberated through my mind: "Purify the vessel." I'd assumed this meant I should continue in my efforts to purify myself, to prepare myself, to make myself worthy. "Purify the vessel." No. There was more to it than that. But, what was it?

The sky became gray as the winter light faded. Scattered streaks of crimson brushed the western horizon. The stillness crystallized around me.

Vessels...

Revelation comes through vessels.

Revelation was like...it was like making wine. Yes. That was it. The grapes are made into juice, but in order for that juice to be saved, preserved, passed from one person to another, it must be put into vessels. We can't hold it in our hands. So we put some into this vessel of teak and some into this vessel of cherry wood, some into this vessel of walnut. And then we wait. Years later, the vessels are opened. We started with the same grapes, with the same pure juice and yet

45

the resulting wines taste quite different. Why? It's impossible for the wine not to take on some of the flavor of the vessel that contains it.

It seemed so clear. God must speak through mortal men and women. The Infinite finds expression as It can, through those who are willing to open themselves to It. And yet, as truth comes through our limited and sometimes prejudiced understandings, it must, of necessity, be colored by our perceptions, our backgrounds, our cultures. No matter how diligently we try, we simply cannot totally separate ourselves from who we are. Spencer W. Kimball was no exception.

This new understanding was real to me. However, I was later to learn that sometimes it takes several lessons on the same theme expressed in various different ways for the meaning to become internalized.

Two years passed.

My assignment had changed since working under Dr. Mason. I was now supervisor over the Church Employment Centers and found myself on my way to San Jose, California. One of my managers had a problem he felt was important enough to require my personal involvement.

When I arrived, he invited me into his office and shut the door. He was seeking direction from his supervisor at Church headquarters in Salt Lake City, and that was me.

"What are we going to do about this job order from Great America?" he asked.

I was familiar with Great America. It was an amusement/recreation park owned by J. Willard Marriott, an extremely prominent and affluent member of the Mormon Church. Having worked for the Marriott Corporation myself both in Washington, D.C., on the industrial relations staff and in Los Angeles, as part of the personnel management team for Marriott Hotels, Inc., I felt a personal connection with Marriott.

"What's the problem?" I asked, wondering why he'd be concerned about job opportunities for his people at a family-oriented place like Great America.

"It's not for regular full-time work," he explained. "It's for temporary work for our sixteen and seventeen-year-old kids for a private party they're having there."

I still couldn't see the problem. "What's wrong, Brother?"

He hesitated. "It's for the GAY NIGHT at the park."

Sometimes it seemed I just could not escape myself. I fought my feelings. I worked at loving Laura and my children and devoting myself to them. I was committed to being the best Bishop I could be. I tried to bury myself in my job. But I just couldn't get away from it. No matter where I went, no matter what I was doing, no matter how I tried to deny it, the truth of my own nature beat in on me, demanding notice, claiming its place.

I concentrated on appearing relaxed and tried to act normal. I couldn't let this Brother see my vulnerability. My heart was hammering and I could feel the uneasy sting of dripping perspiration. I forced the panic away. He didn't know anything about me. He was just asking for my advice as his supervisor. I had to remain calm.

"Deciding what job orders you want or don't want to process is really a local Priesthood decision," I told him. "The decision shouldn't be made by the central headquarters staff. You need to get direction from your regional leaders. They're the parents of the young people who will be directly affected by what you choose."

He nodded. I could see that this made sense to him as well. I knew that if I made the decision for him, it would only come back to haunt me, whichever way I decided. But even more importantly, I knew that my overall purpose as supervisor of the employment centers was to give long-range operational guidance to an entire Church wide system. That meant that what I directed in any one situation would be looked at in the future as precedent should a similar situation ever arise again. I had to consider the international and multi-cultural ramifications of the choices I made. I felt good about my recommendation.

I'd overlooked one thing, however: the power of one tithe-paying cousin of members of the Council of The Twelve, who was also the chairman of the board of his own multi-billion-dollar corporation. Marriott was a man who was used to having his own way. He was a man of political influence in Washington, D.C., and a man who had many favors outstanding with the Corporation of the President, my employer.

Two weeks after returning to my office at Church headquarters, I received a report from the center manager in San Jose. He informed me that the local regional leaders of the Church had decided to cancel all the job orders from Marriott's Great America.

"These brethren," he reported, "don't want their sons and daughters to go there to work and be exposed to displays of affection between people of the same sex." The widely publicized position of the Church on the wrongness of homosexuality had been their justification. "They're afraid," the manager continued, "that some of the youth who have hidden 'tendencies' in that area might have them surface as a result of that kind of exposure. They just don't want to take the risk."

I told him I supported him in his decision. "The Priesthood is what runs the Church," I reiterated, "not someone in the bureaucratic system in Salt Lake City." After all, I understood the doctrine of local Priesthood preeminence over any of the staff bureaucracy employed at headquarters. I had not yet learned a very basic lesson of the Salt Lake City Church headquarters bureaucracy: In spite of all the doctrine, it is in reality only The Twelve Apostles who "run" the Church, not the independent Priesthood leaders in the field, nor any other Priesthood body. I had also forgotten that blood relationships are "thicker than water."

Four days later, my telephone rang. It was my supervisor. "Tony, you have a meeting with Elder _____* of the Council of the Twelve today at 1:00. Be prepared to discuss your decision regarding the Church Employment Center in San Jose."

"Is there something I should know before I go?" I asked.

"No time to discuss it now," he said quickly. "I'm late for a meeting. Come to my office when you're done and I'll fill you in if he doesn't tell you everything."

At 12:50 p.m., I was at the north sub-level security gate to the Church Administration Building in the underground parking lot of the Church Offices complex. I was not really sure what to expect from the upcoming meeting, but I didn't feel especially concerned. I'd handled problems of our staff people many times before. It was part of my job. And I'd been summoned to the offices of others in the uppermost councils of the Church before. It had never caused any problems for me personally.

The guard at the gate knew me and waved me by. Frankly, my mind was on my own problems. It had been the night before that my Stake President had threatened me with the loss of my Church membership if I failed to support him in the proposal he'd made to purchase land owned by his father for use by our Stake. His insults and diatribes still hung bitterly over me.

I could think of nothing that was more important to me than my membership in the Church. This was the one and only true church. I'd devoted my life to it. The threat of losing my connection to all I held most dear was still all I could think of as I got off the elevator and made my way down the plush hallway toward the Apostle's office.

---

* The identity of this member of The Twelve is withheld out of my knowledge that we are all human, after all. It is the actions of one in his Office that are germaine to my story, not his identity.

His secretary greeted me. "Have a seat," she said. "Elder _____ is tied up for a few minutes. He'll be right with you." The door to the inner office was open and I could hear the shuffle of papers. I was so close to the leaders of the Church that maybe sometimes I took them a little for granted. I remembered how for some of the people in Peru, seeing an Apostle was a once-in-a-lifetime experience. I thought of all the humble and sincere converts I had taught when I was a missionary in that country. I remembered their implicit faith in our answers to their questions and their desire to meet the Apostles and Prophets of the Church. I took a seat on the sofa in her office and patiently waited for the Apostle to invite me into his office.

My mind continued to fix itself on the Peruvian members of the Church. It seemed to me that their kind of implicit faith in the leaders of the Church was not unlike that of the ancient ones who had lived in the Early Church of Peter and Paul.

****

It was 1963.

The long black 1957 limousine drove slowly through the crowd of people in downtown Lima just outside the theatre where we'd gathered from throughout the city to greet President Hugh B. Brown, then a member of the First Presidency of the Church. He was there, our mission president had told us earlier, in his capacity as an Apostle of the Lord. I'd traveled into Lima from a nearby poverty-stricken village which had been plunged by a city wide flood into a state of famine, disease, homelessness, and despair.

The humble two-room adobe houses with bamboo doors were gone. Lean-tos made of cardboard, furniture on end, or anything else that could be found, were all that sheltered the shivering people inside from the rain. This is what the members accompanying me had left behind. They wanted to see an Apostle. Very much as the saints of the first century a.d., these were people motivated by a perfect faith in the special mantle of the Spirit which would come with such a man. Without money, or sure accomodations in Lima, these people came to see the man who had come from far-off America, a man who was an Apostle. These were a modern group of saints hoping to meet their own "Saint Paul."

There was an anticipation of the miraculous as the limousine approached. As I overheard conversations around me, I continued to sense over and over that these people waited for President Brown in the same way the early saints must have waited for Peter or Paul as those ancient Apostles traveled the earth bearing witness of Christ, healing the sick, and raising the dead.

As we took our places for the meeting to begin, I sat directly behind a sister I'd been teaching, so that I could help her understand anything the translator missed. However, as President Brown began to speak, I realized that she totally understood everything he said before the translator could even speak. Because of her faith in President Brown and her conviction that he literally was one who spoke for God, she was blessed with the gift of interpretation of tongues. She understood him as clearly as if he'd been speaking her own language.

My experiences with the Twelve had mirrored those of the biblical saints in Acts or the Epistles...

* * * * * * *

And now I waited outside the office of another Apostle. "What a privilege is mine to labor daily with these Prophets of God" I thought to myself.

"Elder _____ will see you now, Brother Feliz."

"So, you're Tony Feliz," he began, nodding a curt greeting and looking me up and down as I took a seat across from him. "And just who, may I ask, gave you the right to set up a personal boycott against Brother Marriott and his entire company?"

"What?" His question startled me. My mind was still in Peru. "Boycott?"

He laughed at my discomfiture. "Why did you get those people in San Jose to stop sending their people to work in his company's park? Who do you think you are anyway?"

"But..." I wasn't prepared for this. I struggled for words to explain.

"Don't you realize I could have your job? I could see you don't ever work for any company related to us in any way ever again! What do you have to say about that?"

"That was a local decision," I protested. "It was a decision made by the local Priesthood leaders."

"Don't tell me anything about local decisions," he snapped back. "You know damn well who runs the Church. We run the Church from up here! So answer me. Why the hell did you do it?"

I glanced uncomfortably toward the the open door, mindful of the secretary just outside.

"I didn't..." I began.

"Of course you did! Aren't you the manager's supervisor from Church headquarters? Damn it, I want an answer and it had better be a good one and not some half-screwed bullshit about local authority."

Was I really hearing this? This man was an Apostle, a member of the Quorum of The Twelve! With the others, he held a special authority to become the Prophet, Seer, and Revelator of the entire Church. He was one of God's anointed, one of God's holy men. Wasn't he? But how could a man who held the keys of the kingdom of God in the way that he did, be acting like this? Cursing, making false accusations, refusing to listen to me? My hands were trembling. I pressed them hard together in my lap, trying to stop the shaking. I was determined to maintain some kind of composure in front of him. I pressed my teeth hard against my tongue, fighting to keep the tears back. I wouldn't let him see me cry. I'd be a man.

Finally, his shouting stopped and I thought he'd let me speak. "You see, Elder _____," I began cautiously, almost afraid he'd interrupt me again, "these regional Priesthood leaders were concerned about their youth coming in contact with public displays of affection between the gay people there that night. They didn't want their sons and daughters to be exposed to something that might trigger tendencies to come to the surface. They were just worried that they'd open up a can of worms by letting their children work at a gay private party. They..."

He shook his head in exasperation. "We're not concerned about the gay thing, you ass! Don't you see you've boycotted the company of a tithe-paying Latter-day Saint, and that's what really matters? You'd better get on the telephone and change your instructions to that employment center today, or I'll see you're tried for your Church membership for disobedience! Do you hear me?"

I stared back at him numbly. I felt like a child who'd been struck viciously by an out-of-control parent for something I hadn't even done. I was helpless and alone and even though a part of me knew it made no sense at all, I still wanted this man's respect and approval.

"I... I'll see it's taken care of," I mumbled.

I couldn't say any more. I couldn't hear any more. "Tried for your Church membership." The words repeated themselves over and over again in my mind—through the secretary's office, along the thickly carpeted hallway, down the elevator, past the security guard, across the underground parking facility—I could not stop their relentless repetition. Why? Why? The question ached from the deepest part of me.

I took another elevator to my office on the eighth floor of the Church Office Building. Only hours before I'd heard the same words from my Stake President. What was happening? I shut the door to my office and sat down at my desk. Nothing seemed real. This couldn't be real. I held my head in my hands. My world was disintegrating around me and there was nothing I could do to stop it. I don't know how long I wept openly with my head on my desk.

Finally, I got up and went to my supervisor's office to report, as he'd requested. He wasn't in; his secretary told me he'd left for the day.

"When did he leave?" I asked.

"Right after he talked to you, I think." She looked at me closely. "Is something wrong, Tony?"

"No. I'm all right. If he calls, tell him I'm sick and I've gone home."

I went back to my office. I dialed the number for the San Jose Employment Center and asked for the manager. "I'm sorry," I said when he answered, "but an authority higher than I has instructed me to reverse my counsel to you on that order from Marriott's Great America. You need to process it right away."

Somehow I got home. After changing clothes I sat in my study and just stared out the window to the east, toward the mountains. I don't know how long I sat there without eating, drinking, or even getting up. I don't remember. Everything was coming unraveled.

And, at last,

When life on earth is through

I will share Eternity with you

--If you love me,

Really love me,

And...

Whatever happens,

I'll be There!

E. Piaf
"Hymne d' Amour"

Chapter 4
Revelation or Administrative Policy?

A frown creased my forehead as I scanned the lines of the letter from Church headquarters. It had arrived in the morning's mail, accompanied by the usual instructions: "Bishops, please share the enclosed letter with the members of your Ward during sacrament meeting." I read the words again, shaking my head.

"What's the matter?" Laura asked, looking up from her book.

I handed her the page and watched while she read quickly through it.

Although I hadn't shared all of my recent frustrations with her, I had told her about my meeting with President Farnsworth and with the Apostle. She knew as well as I did that I had no choice but to read the letter to the Ward, unless I wanted the Stake President to have one more reason to do as he'd threatened.

The letter was from the office of Elder Gordon B. Hinckley, one of the Twelve Apostles. It was a denial that the Church had had anything to do with the anti-Equal Rights Amendment "community" meetings that were currently being held throughout Utah and other crucial E.R.A. politically active areas.

"How can they do this?" I asked Laura. "Laura, you know how they were the ones who told me to ask my Relief Society President to spear-head one of those same meetings as 'a member of her community.' Remember? I showed you the letter!" The women's Relief Society is the Mormon Church's organization with a specific ministry to its adult women.

Laura, as always, was quick to defend the leaders. "They must have a reason, Tony, even if we can't always understand what it is. Their reason must be more important than are we able to see."

"A reason to lie?" The thought of it sickened me. And I was part of it. By standing before my congregation and reading these lies aloud, I condoned them. I was a coward. I'd never really understood why the Church leaders felt such a strong need to fight the Equal Rights Amendment anyway. What were they afraid of? My research at the Church Offices had led me to see that, in the last part of the 1800s, it was the women's movement that had held off the fall of the Church's patriarchy in Utah. It had been the women of Utah that had come to the support of the Church leaders through their independent voting franchise. The reasons given by Church leaders for their fight against the Equal Rights Amendment just did not seem sufficient for their actions.

Laura handed the letter back to me and I started to replace it in the packet with the other information. The Church revered women. "There is no greater calling," I had heard the brethren say over and over, "than to be a wife and mother." It almost seemed sometimes that the leaders felt they were doing women a favor by not allowing them to be equal to men. Protecting them, honoring them, saving them from what men had to deal with. But maybe women didn't want to be protected anymore. Oh, what difference did it make? I was going to read the letter anyway. I glanced down at the signature again. Gordon B. Hinckley. Was he speaking for God? What did God really think about women? Was God against the E.R.A.? I started down the stairs toward my study.

As I passed the door to my sons' bedroom, I stopped. The faint light from the hall reflected off the framed photograph of the Washington, D.C., Temple that hung over the two twin beds. Silhouetted against the sunset, its spires stretched toward heaven.

Revelation or Administrative Policy?

I stepped into the room. Joseph was asleep on his back, one arm thrown above his head. He looked so young, asleep there, the blanket half off him, his breath even and quiet. He stirred as I watched and I tried to pull the blanket smooth over him. I remembered rocking him in our rocker the day he came home. I would never want to teach him anything less than godly truth.

Beside him, in the other bed, only Rafael's head was visible under the tumbled covers. His dark hair was tousled and rough. I brushed it gently away from his forehead and looked back up at the picture on the wall. "What will they think about women?" My thoughts became unnerving: "Will my actions teach something to them that I know is unjust for them to feel about women and equal rights of women?" I needed to find an answer. But, where?

The temple.

Women in the temple. Of course. When I was laboring in the temple in Los Angeles, that had been one of the problems I'd struggled with, one of the questions I'd never been able to find a satisfactory answer to. I remembered writing about it in my journal at the time. I rushed into my study.

I pulled the books from the shelf and thumbed quickly through them until I found the one I wanted. I read what I'd written in 1972:

I don't understand it. It must be one of those areas of the Restored Gospel that I will not get answers to in this life, or so I'm told by other good brethren who labor with me in God's temple. Why are women allowed to authoritatively lay on hands, seal washings and also the anointings, bless others with PRIESTHOOD blessings, etc., without the Priesthood?

All the men are required to be ordained to be allowed to do the same things. The temple president tells me that these women function by virtue of the Priesthood their husbands have. How shallow! What about those sisters who are only set-apart temple ordinance workers who have never been married and who never will get married, much less ordained to some

*order of Priesthood? It just doesn't correlate! It doesn't
compute at all!*

I left the journal open on my desk. I still didn't know
the answers to the questions I'd asked back then. But those
women must have had some kind of Priesthood authority to do
what they did. After all, the ordinances of the temple are the
ordinances of the *fullness* of the Priesthood. Blessing, sealing,
and bestowing power—these were Priesthood functions, but
women were doing them—women who had never been ordained to the Priesthood.

I reached for the dictionary and turned to the O's.
"Ordain." I read Webster's first definition. "to invest officially (as by laying on of hands) with ministerial or sacerdotal
authority." No Mormon scriptorian would have any problem
with that definition. That was exactly the way the word was
always used in Mormon theology. Ordination to the Priesthood was a specific and unalterable bestowal of the authority
by the Church to act in the name of God.

Laura tapped on the partly opened door, then stuck
her head in. "Coming to bed?" she asked.

"Maybe in a minute." She started to leave. "Laura.
Wait. What do you think about women holding Priesthood?"

"What do you mean?" The question had caught her
off guard.

"Do you ever wish you could hold the Priesthood?"

"Of course not. I don't need to."

"Why not?"

"Because you do." It was so clear to her. "We're one,
remember?" She glanced at the books spread out on the desk.
"Don't stay up too late. Good night."

I watched her go. Why couldn't I be more like her?
Her faith simply would not let questions or doubts of any kind
get in its way. Were all the other women in the Church like
her? Did they not feel any need to share the power to act for
God?

I picked up my *Doctrine and Covenants* and flipped
through its well-marked pages. Suddenly, a verse of the

scripture seemed as though it had been lifted up from the page. Bold and vivid, the words stood out as I read them, and I thrilled with the excitement of discovery. I read verses seven and eight...

And thou shalt be ordained under his hand to expound scriptures, and to exhort the church, according as it shall be given thee by my spirit. For he shall lay his hands upon thee and thou shalt receive the Holy Ghost and thy time shall be given to writing, and to learning much.

Joseph Smith was speaking to his wife, Emma Smith! The Lord had revealed the words of Section 25 to her through her husband, the Prophet. Surely Joseph Smith understood the meaning of the word "ordain." There couldn't be any problem with translation here; this revelation had been given in the English language. If God had meant for her to be "set apart" rather than ordained, then why didn't the revelation say it? She'd already been confirmed a member of the Church; she'd received the gift of the Holy Ghost. This obviously referred to something other than a confirmation blessing wherein one receives a command to "receive the Holy Ghost".

I turned to another familiar passage, Section 20, verse 60: *Every elder, priest, teacher, or deacon is to be ordained according to the gifts and callings of God unto him; and he is to be ordained by the power of the Holy Ghost, which is in the one who ordains him.*

Had Joseph been commanded by God to ordain his wife according to the prompting given through him "by the power of the Holy Ghost..in [him]"? But...women couldn't hold the Priesthood! As Laura had said, they didn't need to. But what if the time came when they did need to?

Suddenly, like an instant replay, my mind flashed back to a religion class at Brigham Young University where Dr. Richard L. Bushman had related to us the story of Mary Fielding Smith, the widow of Hyrum Smith and mother of Joseph F. Smith. Her husband had been martyred when his brother, Joseph Smith, was killed. She was traveling across the plains with her family, including a son who would one day become the sixth President of the Mormon Church.

While laboring to pull her heavy wagon across the plains, her oxen collapsed with exhaustion. Laying her hands on the team, she blessed them, whereupon they'd immediately gotten up and continued on the journey without another single problem. Was this done only by faith? Or, was she also a Priesthood member?

I went back to the scripture and reread the verse over and over. But the thought was still too overwhelming. Had Joseph actually ordained these women? Had there been others as well? And if he had, when had the practice stopped? And why?

Through the next week, I spent my lunch hours in the Church Historical Department searching the archives for answers. I soon found myself reading Eliza R. Snow's minutes of the first Relief Society meeting, held in the Red Brick Store in Nauvoo, Illinois:

President Smith further remark'd ... that he would ordain them to preside over the society...President Smith read the revelation to Emma Smith, from the book of Doctrine and Covenants, and stated that she was ordain'd at the time the revelation was given...and that not she alone, but others, may attain to the same blessings.

John Taylor's rendering of his part in this historical event was very carefully recorded in *The Women's Exponent* for September 1, 1880. It supported the other sources.

As I stated, at that meeting, that I was called upon by the Prophet Joseph and I did then ordain Sisters Whitney and Cleveland, and blessed Sister Emma and set her apart. I could not ordain these sisters to anything more or to greater powers than had been conferred upon Sister Emma who had previously been ordained.

There seemed no question but that women had been ordained. But why had the practice been discontinued? Would women ever have this blessing again? And if it was to be, how would the revelation come? A talk in conference? A new section of scripture in the *Doctrine and Covenants*? A press conference? Why did it seem to me that something very much like this had already happened?

But, of course. There had been another group of oppressed people who had been denied these same blessings...

* * * * * * *

It was June 1978.

The telephone in my office rang. It was a member of my Ward who worked in the Church Public Communications Department. He was breathless and excited. "Bishop, have you heard the news?"

"What news?"

"President Kimball has received a revelation and has authorized that the Blacks can now receive the Priesthood!" He began to read the official letter of announcement to me.

My eyes filled with tears. There had been bonds restricting the full flow of power the earth was capable of. They were being loosened. Light was being allowed to enter where before there had been darkness. I was a part of this opening, this unfolding, this beginning again. I was overwhelmed with it.

"Is there another document?" I asked. "I mean, is there a written revelation the Brethren are going to release?"

"No. This is it. This is the official announcement."

All day my phone rang. Why the calls came to me I didn't know. I worked in Welfare Services; I wasn't connected to the Public Communications Department in any way. But the calls and questions didn't stop. Was it true? Why had it happened now? How had President Kimball received the "revelation"? Why had Brigham Young taught that the Blacks wouldn't be able to receive the Priesthood until everyone else had received it first? Did this mean that the Black members of the Church could now go to the temples and receive their full temple blessings?

Out of the Bishop's Closet

I had answered them all as well as I could...

* * * * * * *

Back in my study, I kept coming up with more "unanswerable" questions. I put the dictionary in its place and closed my journal. Joseph Smith had ordained Blacks to the Priesthood. I'd read journals attesting to it. Why had Brigham Young discontinued the practice? And how would the members of the Church react if a similar "revelation" were to be received today about women? A revelation stating that now every worthy member of the Church could hold the Priesthood? But it wouldn't be. Not yet, anyway. We weren't ready. But that wasn't even the real issue. The problem was that the doctrine had been changed. I couldn't understand why. And if this doctrine had been changed, for whatever reason, were there others as well? Were there other truths we were depriving ourselves of because of our closed minds, our unwillingness to see things as they were?

The very idea was enough to send indescribable sensations of fear throughout my whole body. Where were all these questions leading me?

On Sunday, I read the letter to my congregation at the beginning of the sacrament service. This letter from one of the Twelve Apostles didn't seem important to others. No one paid any attention. Was I the only person troubled by Elder Hinkley's apparently false denials?

I finished the business portion of the meeting. Announcing the sacrament hymn, I gave some usual counsel. I reminded those gathered that the reason for our meeting was to join in worshiping our Father in Heaven. I reminded them of the covenants they'd all made when they were baptized and challenged them to let this be a time of renewal for them, a time when those promises could be made once again with sincerity and humbleness of heart.

Revelation or Administrative Policy?

The chapel grew quieter as two of our young men stood to break the bread. The way we worshiped seemed so natural to me. From my childhood, this was the way Church had been. This pattern, this form, this order. But today my mind was full of questions. Did it need to be this way? How important was it to do things in this particular order, in this specific way? Did it matter when we prayed, or if one prayed or all prayed together? Or what kind of music we had or if we had music at all? Was this just one more instance of our accepting what was "comfortable," rather than what was true? Hadn't many of these decisions been left up to those who'd been ministers in other churches before joining the early Mormon Church? How had we let ourselves get so locked into things that were so obviously only cultural? So obviously not revealed, but yet, looked upon as if they had been.

I looked out over my Ward members and remembered the love I'd had for all of them before I'd even known them. I knew them all so well now. They were good people, honest people, loving people that wanted the best for themselves and their children. Most of them were trying hard to do what they felt they were supposed to be doing. They looked to me for guidance. They came to me with their questions and their worries, their doubts, and their pain. And their sins. The men were embarrassed and apologetic. The women cried. The children always looked up at me with a kind of awe as they pressed their worn and grubby tithing envelopes into my hands.

How could I lead them when I had so many questions of my own? There was so much that, for me, just didn't seem to add up.

The words came clearly into my mind, "Think not of what you do not know, but rather of what you do." Sometimes I felt as if I didn't know anything anymore.

I knew that Joseph Smith was a Prophet of God. I knew that God had reached out and touched this man, and that the world had been forever changed by the light of that connection. I thought of the Prophet laying his hands on his wife's head and ordaining her to the Priesthood. There must have been many things Joseph had tried to teach that the people of his day simply were not ready to accept or understand.

I was daring now to ponder these questions.

Prophets can't speak in a vacuum. All that they say must be said within the context they live in. In the Jacksonian era of U.S. history when Mormonism had its nativity, most Blacks were still slaves and women were considered "the weaker sex," almost a possession to be owned and controlled just as the slaves were.

Why should it be surprising that the prevailing attitudes changed and shaped the doctrines Joseph tried to teach? He'd tried desperately to get the Church to rise above its time and society. And what happened? The society he lived in killed him for his efforts. My mind went off to another place where I had been...

****

It was 1978.

I'd already seen 19th-century journals with these experiences recorded in them. My research in the Church Historical Department had already taught me much. I was on a flight high above the Andes Mountains in South America. I was on assignment for the Welfare Services of the Church. I accompanied Elder William R. Bradford, a member of the First Quorum of The Seventy of the Church. This is the administrative body next in authority to the Apostles and Prophets of the Church. I was expressing some of these doctrinal dilemmas to him. "Elder Bradford," I asked, "how is it that the theologies of the Prophets of the Church in the last century are so different from that of our Prophets today?"

"Tony," he answered, "the eternal principles of the revelations are interpreted in the practice of the Church."

Revelation or Administrative Policy?

"Do you mean that the principles can be manifested in different policy depending on the age and the society of the people?" I was totally taken by his statement.

"Yes, Tony."

I continued to relate to him what I'd found in the historical documents that I had been exposed to while working in the Church Offices and he added, "Another way to say it might be: revelation is manifest in the policy of the Church."

Somehow, this helped, but I was still not totally satisfied. I felt that if indeed the Prophets were receiving direction directly from a Divine Source, then the policy of the Church would be the only changing factor. It seemed to me that what I had observed was a definite pattern change in the theology as well. That was when I first began to wonder how one distinguishes mere administrative policy from revealed instruction.

* * * * * * *

The sacrament was over. Most of the young men returned to sit with their families and I went to the pulpit to announce the rest of the meeting, then took my seat again. Usually I tried to look out at all the members as the speakers shared their insights and testimonies. Often, it seemed this was the way God alerted me to a person or a family who had a special need. As I scanned the congregation, it would be almost as if these people were the only ones I could see clearly. They would stand out distinctively from the others and I'd know that I needed to see them individually or to pray for further guidance to know what their inner needs were.

My family sat on the third row. Lynne was on Laura's lap. Joseph and Rafael sat on each side of her. The rest of the congregation faded. I wanted to reach out to my family, but they were too far away. I felt as if I were seeing them from a great distance, and their forms were blurring and changing as they moved farther and farther away from me. The reality of the separation wrenched at me. I was powerless to stop it.

In an effort to communicate, I formed the fingers on my right hand in the deaf sign for "I love you" to Rafael. He and Joseph both returned the sign.

Such joy they were! I knew I loved them.

I wanted to be worthy of Laura's love, of her faith, her strength. I didn't want to be gay. Why did I have to feel the way I did? I'd prayed. I'd fasted. I'd tried in every way I knew to purge myself, to make myself pure. But I couldn't. Why?

These two men sitting on either side of me were so good. Why couldn't I just love my counselors as my brothers? These two men were honest, honorable, and faithful men. Why did I feel such a strong draw, such a yearning when I was around them? I knew that what I felt toward them came from deep within me, and I knew that it was wrong in the eyes of the Church. But, it was real and powerful, nevertheless. Why wasn't I delivered from this pain?

Somehow, I got through all my meetings.

Sundays were busy. It was always late when the last meeting was over, the last interview finished. It was after nine and the children were already sleeping when Laura brought my dinner to me.

"You didn't have to do this," I said, not getting up from the couch. I hadn't turned on the lamp and the quiet darkness was warm and welcome.

"I know." She sat down near me, and I started to eat.

"Do you want to talk about it?" she asked.

I feigned surprise "About what?"

"Tony," she said, with just the barest hint of exasperation at the edges of her voice, "you've hardly come out of your office for days. When you do, you act as if you're a million miles away. Today at church, you were looking at us like you were afraid you'd never see us again." Her fingers brushed my leg. "I need to know what's going on." She didn't say the "please" aloud, but her voice was full of it.

Revelation or Administrative Policy?

Please, please, tell me what's going on. Don't pull away from me like this. Don't separate yourself from me.

Could I tell her? Could I give form to the uneven clash of my recent thoughts? Would she understand? I had to try.

I set the half-eaten plate of food aside and took her two hands in mine in the darkened room. I had my own unspoken pleas. *Please, please listen to me. Please try to understand. Please don't condemn me.*

"Do you remember," I began carefully, "when I was working on that 'Wasatch Front' project at work? When we were trying to determine what parts of the traditional Mormon lifestyle were really part of the gospel, and not just things that had been part of our local 'Wasatch Front' subculture for so long that we thought they were necessary to live the gospel?"

She nodded, confused at why I should be concerned now about this study I'd worked on so long ago. "I remember. What about it? Tony, that was years ago. What's wrong?"

Maybe she would understand! "You see, the problem was that a lot of newly converted members of the Church in very poor areas of the world felt that when they joined the Church, they had to copy the lifestyle of 'Wasatch-Front-Utah-Valley' Mormons- who'd taught them the gospel. These new faithful just did not have any of the resources to support that kind of a change in lifestyle. When the leaders saw what was happening, they began to realize that there might be other things as well, things we were sort of unconsciously teaching as part of the gospel that really weren't.

Our assignment was to separate those out."

"But is it really possible to do that?"

"I remember once we were in a meeting talking about all of this. I asked everyone if it was important for the priests to wear white shirts and ties when they blessed the sacrament even if they would be the only ones in the entire congregation to dress that way. Some of the people there thought they should. Others didn't feel it would be that important."

69

"Oh, I see." In her usual perceptive way, Laura grasped at once the relevance of this to what I'd just said. "The important thing was that they came prepared to worship, wearing whatever they needed in order to help them create the right feeling. White shirts and ties are what make us feel worshipful. It might be something altogether different for someone from another place."

"Then I asked them another question. I asked them how different that situation would be from the priest of a Catholic Church who dresses in fourth-century robes when he officiates at a mass in a twentieth-century church."

"But I think the Catholic priests sort of want to set themselves apart from the people."

"Exactly. But do we?"

She realized it was not a question that needed an answer. In the Mormon tradition, even temple Priesthood vestments have an intrinsic purpose of manifesting the unity of all Church members, rather than that of setting some apart from the rest.

"So what happened? What did you decide?"

"Well, a lot of things happened. We realized that in some areas of the world where public meetings are forbidden by the government it's not really that important for the members to have regularly scheduled meetings each Sunday. We realized that testimony meetings don't have to be the first Sunday of each month, that they can be held any time. We realized that a lava lava was an entirely appropriate thing for a man to wear to church in Samoa, and that if a congregation in the south liked to repeat 'Amen' aloud whenever they heard something they agreed with, then that was all right too."

"Okay," she said slowly, trying to see where all this was leading. "But what does this have to do with us? Why do..." She hesitated to put her fear into words. "Why do I feel you're so far away from me, Tony?"

"I just think that maybe there are many more things like that, things we didn't ever really think about when we were doing that study—ideas, practices, and concepts that are taught in the Church as doctrine, but are really just sort of...well, administrative policy. Someone up in Church head-quarters makes a decision to do something a certain way and pretty soon it's accepted as revealed truth."

I reminded her of the time I personally had authored a draft of a letter that was to go out to all Priesthood leaders of the Church over the signatures of the First Presidency. I had her recall that even though none of the First Presidency was in their offices that day, I had secured all three of their signatures through the use of a signature machine in their offices. My letter had been accepted by the entire body of the Church's Priesthood as if from the Prophet's own pen! Its instructions had become veritable scripture to them even though the Prophets, themselves, had never even seen the letter.

"I don't think that happens very often," she objected. "Besides, would it really hurt anyone if it did? I mean, aren't those leaders making their decisions after praying and talking it over with each other and considering all the information they have available anyway?"

She couldn't see my point. It wasn't the small, day-to-day administrative decisions that mattered so much. It was simply annoying when those kinds of directions were taken as revelation, but not disastrous. Wearing a tie or not wearing one was not going to destroy anyone's life. "No, Laura," I tried to explain, "it's more than that." I wanted so much for her to see. I wanted someone to share this struggle with me. "In the middle of the nineteenth century, Brigham Young kept people from getting their temple ordinances out of an economically based decision: 'Anyone found to be trucking with the Gentiles will not receive a recommend to the Endowment House' he said. Laura, that meant that some people would not receive their necessary temple ordinances because of some economic boycotting, not because of a person's individual worthiness."

Laura still couldn't see my perspective.

She wouldn't see.

"I know I've been pretty distant this last while. I'm sorry. I've been trying to figure some things out. I need to find out for myself what's true, what's finally and absolutely true, not just what we think is true and accept as true because of our culture and our background and what we're used to. I want to strip all the filters away."

"You used to know what was true," she said gently, not really condemning, but almost. "What is it you don't know anymore?"

I took a deep breath. "Oh, like women in the Church," I suggested.

"Women? What about women?"

"Maybe the whole attitude of the Church toward women is mostly just cultural. Women used to not be able to pray in Sacrament Meeting. Now they can. They can't hold Priesthood now. Maybe someday they will."

Laura shook her head in frustration. "How can you say that?" she began, then stopped, realizing there was no way she could make me understand her viewpoint either. "Are there other things too?"

I hesitated. "Maybe the Church's official position on...on...homosexuality."

"On what?" I had said the offending word so softly she could barely hear me.

I repeated it.

She looked at me in total amazement. "Why would you care about that?" She paused. "You're not trying to tell me you think it's all right to do that, to be that way, are you? Are you?"

I still didn't answer.

"Tony, that's perverted! It's...it's..." But she couldn't find words strong enough to express her revulsion.

There was a word for her fear, a word I'd only learned recently myself: "homophobia." A vague, unreasonable fear of gay and lesbian people coupled with a confused notion that homosexuality must somehow be contagious. A fear that unless you are totally and overtly against homosexuality in any form, you'll be treated the same way homosexuals are—hated, falsely accused, discriminated against by the rest of society.

72

Revelation or Administrative Policy?

If only she'd try to understand. If only everyone could. We're only afraid when we don't understand.

"Maybe we just don't understand it," I persisted. "Maybe if we did, we'd see it's like the other things. Joseph Smith never said anything against it."

I'd searched the writings of Joseph Smith to see what he taught. He said this: "*Our Heavenly Father is more liberal in his views, and boundless in his mercies and blessings, than we are ready to believe or receive.*" What would he have taught if he'd been free to share all he knew? If he hadn't had to limit himself to the doctrines that the society he was in would accept?

"It probably wasn't the problem then it is now," Laura offered. "That's why Joseph Smith didn't talk about it."

But I knew that wasn't the case. I thought of John Bennett, an acknowledged homosexual, whom The Prophet had made mayor of Nauvoo and the assistant president of the Church after discovering Bennett's homosexuality. I thought to myself, "If Joseph Smith had wanted to speak out against homosexuality, what better opportunity could he have asked for than when all the controversy about Bennett finally surfaced?" But, I didn't verbalize any of this.

"I think it was," I said lamely.

"But we have a Prophet today, Tony, and he has said something about it." She shifted nervously on the couch. "Why are you worrying about all this now anyway? Did something just happen that's made you start thinking about this?"

Why couldn't I say it? Why couldn't I just say, "Laura, I'm gay. I love you and I love our children, and I don't want to do anything to hurt you or them, but all my yearnings, my dreams, my most secret unspoken longings are for men"?

But there was no way I could tell her. "It's just hard for me," I hedged, "when we have to have Church courts on these guys who admit they're gay. It's hard for me to condemn them."

73

"Oh, that's it." She was visibly relieved. "Bishops have to mingle with the sinners."This she could relate to. It was all right to care about others who had sinned, to be concerned, even a little overwhelmed. Bishops' wives had to accept the fact that they shared their husbands with hundreds of other people.

"Just remember you don't have to carry the burden of the whole world alone," she whispered. "That's what I'm here for. Let me share it with you."

I reached to touch her cheek. Sometimes I felt I didn't deserve this woman. "Laura," I said softly, "I love you."

As we sat there on the sofa together in the darkness, I began to wonder what the future would hold for my two daughters. What kind of life will they have in our Mormon society that now was beginning to seem to me to be very repressive to women. Will Lynne and Raquel grow up to experience all that they are capable of? When I thought of those possibilities, my mind kept on going back to Emma Hale Smith, Mary Fielding Smith and Eliza R. Snow, the early Mormon women who'd been so powerful and dynamic in their impact on the Church. Will my two daughters have the chance to experience the same kind of strength and vitality that was exhibited by such women of the early days of Mormonism? If not, why not? I wanted the best for my girls. If the women of Joseph Smith's day were helped in their spiritual service by Priesthood ordination, why couldn't my daughters also have this blessing?

During the ensuing year, I capitalized on some friendships I'd made with employees in the Church Historian's Office and returned to the archives. This time I needed to find answers for myself and I needed to use all the resources at my disposal. I needed to know, especially now, the history—or evolution—of the current position of the Church on homosexuality.

That which is wrong under one circumstance, may be, and often is right under another.

God said, 'Thou shalt not kill;' at another time He said, 'Thou shalt utterly destroy.' This is the principle on which the government of heaven is conducted--by revelation adapted to the circumstances in which the children of the kingdom are placed...If we seek first the kingdom of God, all good things will be added...even things which might be considered abominable to all who understand the order of heaven only in part, but which in reality were right...

This principle will justly apply to all of God's dealings with His children. Everything that God gives us is lawful and right...

The Prophet Joseph Smith
August 27, 1842
Documentary History of the Church
Vol. 5:134-136

Chapter 5
Into The Church Archives

As I sat on the stand waiting for our sacrament meeting to begin, I noticed a good-looking man, and his wife, and five little ones walk into the chapel from the outer foyer. Jeff and Irene were new members of our Ward, and somehow I knew as I saw them come into the chapel that first Sunday that, in Jeff, I was looking at a kindred spirit. Here was another soul who had suffered, maybe even more than I had.

After the meeting, I was sure to introduce myself to them. As I shook hands with Jeff, I could tell that he was wondering if he could share a major need in his life with me, his new Bishop. "I hope we become good friends," I said. He didn't answer, but the look he gave me let me know that this was his hope as well.

It was not long until Jeff came over to my home to share with me the need I'd sensed in our first meeting. Several years before, Jeff had been tried before a Church court and he had been excommunicated for homosexual practices. Before they'd joined our Ward, he'd been accepted back into the Church and had been rebaptized. Jeff told me that he had forsaken his homosexual life and that he wanted to return to the temple with his wife and be allowed to function once again in the Church as an Elder in the Priesthood.

Having gone through this process before with others seeking to conform to requirements of full fellowship within

77

the Mormon Church, I knew what needed to be done. My colleagues in the Confidential Section of the Presiding Bishopric's Office understood that the Priesthood was separate from the Church. They had informed me that, since Jeff had previously received the sacred ordinances of the temple, he still had the Priesthood, and there was no need to reordain him to that higher order; he only needed to have his Priesthood and temple blessings restored, in a simple laying-on-of-hands blessing by a person in authority to do this.

"I've never understood this idea," Jeff confessed in one of our talks. "Bishop, what does it really mean to have your temple blessings restored?"

"You don't need to be reordained or reinitiated in the temple," I explained. "Nothing done in the temple can be terminated by a Church court, because Church courts have no jurisdiction in the temple. Excommunication can keep a member outside of the temple, but it can't nullify the ordinances that were conferred there. When you go to the temple, you receive an "endowment" of knowledge and keys. That's a gift, a blessing that can't be taken from you by any person or institution, although perhaps the right to use it within an institution might be. By restoring your Priesthood and temple blessings, the Church isn't giving them back to you. You've had them all along. It's only saying that it acknowledges once again your right to use them within the organization we call the Church.

Jeff's situation stimulated my interest in the roots of the current Church administrative procedure regarding its homosexual faithful. When did the early Church leaders begin to excommunicate gay people? What did Joseph Smith have to say about gays? Who had received revelations on this issue?

Though very nervous, I went into the archives, I began my own search for answers. I pretended I wanted to know because of Jeff, because I wanted to understand why the Church took the theological stand it did on homosexuality, so

I could explain it to him. But, deep down, I knew that I was really looking for answers for myself. Sometimes, although I knew it was ridiculous, I was afraid that everyone around could see what I was reading, and that somehow by seeing it they would know that I was gay. I was very careful not to let anyone know the subject of my research. These people in the Historical Department of the Church Offices were my friends. I kept filling up with self-imposed guilt for even searching out information on the subject. I felt as if it were wrong even to question.

As I studied, I became more and more distressed by one particular doctrine, a doctrine seemingly at the very heart of Mormonism: the Mormon view of heaven and the concept of God.

It began with a sermon of the Prophet Joseph Smith, the King Follett Sermon. Long criticized by non-Mormons as not having been correctly recorded because most accounts were not compiled until roughly ten years after it had been delivered, this sermon has become basic to Mormon theology. From it, the Church has developed the dogma that in the resurrection man may become a God "the Father" and woman a "Heavenly Mother," This exaltation is impossible unless the two are completely and inseparably joined—married on earth for Eternity. I discovered the traditional Mormon belief in an anthropomorphic God—a human god that had to be a male who had a female—was at the root of the entire current theology which left homosexual life, no matter how conservative or adherent to Christian values, totally locked out of Holy Temples.

I read what Brigham Young had taught.

He created man, as we create our children; for there is no other process of creation in heaven, on the earth, or under the earth, or in all the eternities, that is, that were, or that ever will be. Journal of Discourses 11:122

Journals, diaries, conference reports, and minutes of meetings all revealed to me that, through the generations that followed Brigham Young, this concept continued to expand until the conclusion was reached that if children were born to God in the same manner that they were born to mankind, there must also be a "Heavenly Mother" somewhere that was party to the creation in addition to the Godhead mentioned in the scriptures.

I found what John A. Widstoe had written in his book, *A Rational Theology*, when he was a member of the Council of The Twelve had contributed to the evolution of this now traditional Mormon concept...

Sex, which is indispensable on this earth for the perpetuation of the human race, is an eternal quality which has its equivalent elsewhere. It is indestructible. The relationship between men and women is eternal and must continue eternally.

In accordance with gospel philosophy, there are males and females in heaven. Since we have a Father, who is our God, we must also have a Mother, who possesses the attributes of Godhood.

This statement did not seem to purport to be a revealed statement, a revelation from God. Wasn't it just a statement of belief made by a member of the Twelve who was trying to elucidate on established and accepted teachings by other individuals in sermons, writings, and classes? But, this idea was what everyone now believed. Heterosexual procreation had become the means that most Mormons accepted for what Joseph Smith called "eternal increase" in the hereafter.

I read the statement again. Elder Widstoe had used the words "its equivalent" in referring to the process of procreation "elsewhere." He knew that many organisms do use other processes besides the one we as humans use to procreate.

One day, a strange thought struck me. Why should heterosexual intercourse be the only process of "increase" in heaven? I began to review the documentation on the evolution of this theology of "eternal increase." I looked in the scriptures first. Nowhere was the process of "eternal increase" in eternity identified as procreation; the scriptures only taught that "eter nal increase" did exist in the highest degree of what Mormons call the Celestial Kingdom.

I found that the King Follett Sermon by Joseph Smith did not state that heterosexual intercourse was the process of becoming a being with "eternal increase" or becoming a god. All this sermon did was claim that God was an "exalted man who sits enthroned in yonder heavens." It didn't even say that God, as traditional Mormon belief today states, had a body of flesh and bones. It did say that if someone were to see God as He is now, He would be seen as a man, in the form and likeness of a man. I reasoned to myself, though, that such an appearance wouldn't, in itself, be sufficient to claim that God's form was a body of flesh and bones. I asked myself why it couldn't be something else. Why couldn't God's form be made of a more refined matter than flesh and bones? Then, it would fit into Joseph's other written statements. Joseph Smith had dictated the words found in the *Book of Mormon* which declare in speaking of spirits in final resurrection as *"...spirits uniting with their bodies, never to be divided; thus the whole becoming spiritual and immortal, that they can no more see corruption."* (Alma 11:45) I began to wonder where the idea of God having "a body of flesh and bones as tangible as man's" was first recorded.

I realized I was treading dangerously. It was frightening to me even to consider that such a basic theology to my Church was one that I had begun to question. After all, Joseph Smith was supposed to have said in the King Follett Sermon that the first principle of revealed religion is to know the character and nature of God.

Then, I found that the only document published when Joseph Smith was still alive which stated a definition—as we have access to it today—of the character or attributes of God was in the *Lectures on Faith*. Unfortunately, these had been deleted from Mormon scripture by the leaders after they had come out to Utah. In the first edition of the *1835 Doctrine and Covenants*, Joseph Smith published this definition by writing:

"There are two personages who constitute the great, matchless, governing and supreme power over all things...They are the Father and the Son: The Father being a personage of spirit, glory and power; The Son, who was in the bosom of the Father, a personage of tabernacle...the express image and likeness of the personage of the Father..." Doctrine and Covenants, 1835 edition pages 52-53.

I was stunned.

Could it be? Why had it been removed? There was no mention of a body of flesh and bones, yet this was published long after Joseph Smith's famous vision wherein he saw two personages. Then, it hit me. These were never described by Joseph Smith as personages of *flesh and bones*. That is when I began to realize that historical documents in Mormonism are journals, diaries, minutes of meetings, and the like. Joseph Smith rarely (if ever) actually wrote down anything himself, the exception being his personal letters to Emma, his wife. All else historians used to decipher his communications were documents actually penned by others. The source in the case of the concept if God's body being made of "flesh and bones" was actually recorded by Church historians as being William Clayton, not Joseph Smith. Joseph had always referred to Them as beings of *glory*, beings of *light*. My mind couldn't forget the day in my seminary class when, as an adolescent, I'd learned that Joseph Smith had taught that spirit is actually matter, that it is more refined than matter as we mortals understand matter to be. I began to question another commonly quoted Mormon scripture from the *Doctrine and Covenants*. It was a scripture stating flatly that *"The Father has a body of flesh and bones as tangible as man's...."* I began to wonder who really wrote that verse. It was the only written statement that seemed to say outrightly that God the Father had a body of flesh and bones. I began to distrust the early leaders after Joseph's death. I began to doubt that this small statement actually originated with Joseph Smith.

It didn't add up. Why would the Prophet Joseph Smith have changed his concept of The Father? Why?

Into the Church Archives

I returned again and again to the scripture that some point to as their "proof" that Joseph Smith taught that heterosexual intercourse was the means of procreation in heaven: *Doctrine and Covenants* 131:2: *"In the celestial glory there are three heavens or degrees; And in order to obtain the highest, a man must enter into this order of the priesthood [meaning the new and everlasting covenant of marriage]."* It seemed to me that what Joseph was trying to explain was that there is an order of Priesthood that was required in order to enter the "highest" heaven.

The question still remained: Did that Priesthood order absolutely require that "marriage" be its prerequisite; and if not, who inserted the parenthetical statement, and why?

Burt was an employee of the Church Historian's Office with whom I'd become friends. I asked Burt, "Is that parenthetical statement original to the revelation or was it added for purposes of clarification later by the Brethren?"

"I don't think there's any way we can tell, Tony."

"Why not?"

"The original is not available to us. The First Presidency has it on the restricted list. There's no way for us to see. Now that you bring it up, Tony; it is interesting that these 'items of instruction' were never published in Joseph Smith's lifetime."

"And" I thought to myself, "what were recorded as 'items of instruction' may not be as final as what we called 'revelation'."

It just didn't fit into the rest of the stuff we'd gotten through Joseph Smith. This statement seemed more like something that would come from the pen of Brigham Young or a contemporary in Utah during the post Joseph Smith years.

I went back to the published revelations. The revelation the Church accepted as from Joseph Smith, in *Doctrine and Covenants* 132, stuck in my mind. It was the final statement on exactly what is entailed in what Joseph Smith spoke of as "The New and Everlasting Covenant." The leaders of the Mormon Church now taught that heterosexual marriage in the temple is the "highest" order of Priesthood spoken of in these sections of the *Doctrine and Covenants*. But was it? What if the New and Everlasting Covenant was really much broader than heterosexual marriage? I read section 132 again; it was a revelation that Joseph Smith had originated...

And as pertaining to the new and everlasting covenant...the conditions of this law are these: All covenants, contracts, bonds, obligations, oaths, vows, performances, connections, associations, or expectations... Doctrine and Covenants 132:6-7

I read further. The revelation went on to state that in order for any of those kinds of relationships mentioned to exist beyond the grave, they needed to be sealed upon the parties involved. Was it possible that it was an all-encompassing covenant, a promise that literally included every aspect of human living? Maybe Joseph Smith really did envision his followers in a future society who would seek for a special sealing blessing of the Holy Spirit of Promise on all relationships so that those relationships could reach beyond the grave.

Sometimes as I read and studied, I wondered if I was just trying to rationalize my sinfulness. Was I trying to twist the words of the scriptures into what I wanted them to say so that I would no longer feel condemned? At other times it seemed so clear that what the Church was teaching today was now vastly different from the gospel as Joseph Smith had taught it. It was becoming very clear to me that the founding Prophet of Mormonism was a prophet in the classic sense. Joseph Smith was evidently not the origin of all the homophobic commentary which had crept into the Church of today. His gospel was liberal enough, simple enough, and inclusive enough to save and exalt every kind of people.

Into the Church Archives

I found that Joseph began a practice of sealing men to men during the last two years of his life in Nauvoo. Many of the journals, letters, and other materials I researched recorded accounts of these sealings of men to men. This practice had continued until 1894, when Wilford Woodruff stopped the practice of the ordinance because Brigham Young had made *"changes"* in the ordinance and *"more revelation"* was needed before it could be resumed again (*Millenial Star*, Vol. 56, pages 337-341). Had this been a son-to-father kind of sealing? It seemed that by the time it was discontinued that's what it had become. But, the more I researched, the more convinced I became that, in the days of Joseph Smith, the sealing of men had not necessarily been mere sealings of sons to fathers. In speaking of the Salt Lake Temple then under construction, Brigham Young taught, *"Men will be sealed to men in the priesthood."* Journal of Discourses 16:1868

What did all this mean?

I found that during the days Joseph had initiated the practice in Nauvoo, he said, while preaching a funeral sermon:

It is my meditation all the day & more than my meat and drink to know how I shall make the saints of God to comprehend the visions that roll like an overflowing surge, before my mind...it is pleasing for friends to lie down together locked in the arms of love to sleep, & locked in each others embrace awake & renew their conversation. Joseph Smith diary, 16 April 1843

I broke out in a cold sweat. Joseph Smith had said that? His statement didn't sound very platonic to me! This funeral sermon had been for several people. Among those being remembered was a man named Lorenzo Barnes and the wife of a man named Marcellus Bates. Brother Bates was present in the congregation, as well as a person whom Joseph had referred to earlier as *"the friend of Lorenzo Barnes."* I read what the Prophet had lovingly said to the two who were mourning the loss of their respective loved ones:

...when others rejoice I rejoice. when they mourn I would mourn—

to Marcellus Bates, let me administer comfort, you shall soon have the company of your companion in a world of glory—& the friend of Brother Barns... Joseph Smith Diary, kept by Willard Richards, 16 April 1843.

Could Joseph Smith really have here been including a private relationship between Lorenzo Barns and his *"friend"* in the same category as that of Marcellus Bates and his wife? It seemed impossible, but there it was. What if his *"friend"* was a man?

Wilford Woodruff had been present that day too, and had also recorded his memory of the sermon in his journal:

Two who were vary [sic] *friends indeed should lie down upon the same bed at night locked in each other's embrace talking of their love & should awake in the morning together that they could immediately renew their conversation of love even while rising from their bed...* Wilford Woodruff Journal, 16 April 1843

Conversation of love? It didn't seem there was any way that could be taken metaphorically. Was there? And even if Joseph hadn't meant these statements to be construed to mean that same-sex unions could be solemnized by the Priesthood at the sacred altars of the temple, there was certainly nothing homophobic about them. Indeed, they were far removed from the rhetoric given today over Church pulpits in light of the intimate love I'd sensed could be deeply felt between men.

Joseph was sealing men to men. He was saying it was good for friends to lie down together locked in each other's arms and to awaken in each other's embrace. Could it have been that he was trying to give the saints of his day a broader view of heaven than they were ready to receive? What was it he'd said once? It was one of the most significant quotations from Joseph Smith that I'd ever seen. Burt had told me that this specific statement had been written under the specific direction of Joseph Smith, unlike the other documentation which had actually been recorded by others as he spoke. I found the place again in the *Teachings of The Prophet Joseph Smith*, on page 257:

> *That which is wrong under one circumstance, may be and often is, right under another. God said, "Thou shalt not kill;" at another time He said, "Thou shalt utterly destroy."*
>
> *This is the principle on which the government of heaven is conducted—by revelation adapted to the circumstance in which the children of the kingdom are placed...If we seek first the kingdom of God, all good things will be added...even things which might be considered abominable to all who understand the order of heaven only in part, but which in reality are right...*
>
> *This principle will justly apply to all of God's dealings with His children. Everything that God gives us is lawful and right...*
>
> *Our heavenly Father is more liberal in His views, and boundless in His mercies and blessings, than we are ready to believe or receive...*August 27, 1842, Documentary History of The Church 5:134-136 (Author's emphasis added)

It seems now, looking back, that these discoveries should've given me comfort, that they should've helped me in my struggle to accept myself. But strangely, they didn't. I still felt a great love for the Church and as I found and studied historical documents that seemed to contradict what the Church taught, I only felt more confused. My inner selves still argued and fought, striving against each other in a battle it seemed would never end.

I loved the Church.

From childhood, for me, it had been the fountain of all that I'd ever held dear. The Church had given me a reason to excell in my personal education and in my career. The Church was my main motivator in maintaining myself free of drugs and alcolol during my growing up years in the sixties. The Church had been the significant reason that I now had a wonderful and loving wife and four beautiful children. The Church was that one thing in our society that seemed to be able to hold up answers to all my questions throughout my life's experience. All of them, that is, but one. As the time for General Conference drew nearer, I hoped that perhaps it would bring me some peace.

But, there was another problem. My research uncovered some facts of life that I was not ready to see. Reading the minutes of meetings held by the First Presidencies, the Twelve Apostles and the Presiding Bishoprics of the Church revealed much of a side of these leaders to me that I'd never acknowledged before. These men were very human. They fought terrible battles with one another in these council meetings over issues which they each felt very strongly about. I, somehow, hadn't ever imagined that Apostles—holy men— ever argued in their council meetings. I had carried the misconception that all was "revelation" for them. It was quite a discovery, for me to see them in these minutes as human beings laboring with one another in a political fashion in order to get each other to understand their individual opinions and views. I hadn't realized it, but I was experiencing somewhat of a spiritual culture shock.

I had not yet internalized the thought that had come to me a few years earlier, that Prophets are human beings, after all.

I sat in a section of the Salt Lake Tabernacle reserved for Bishoprics, Stake Presidencies, Patriarchs, and Regional Representatives of the Priesthood as I waited for the next session to begin. I could hear the whispered conversation of my Stake Presidency from directly behind me.

I especially needed an uplift today. I needed the spiritual regeneration I knew Conference could bring. General Conference had always been an oasis of spiritual feeding for me, a source of strength from which I could leave with an energized renewal of fervor for the work of the Church. I just wanted to forget all the rest of what was happening around me: President Farnsworth's accusations, Elder _____'s threats, my frustrating research that either didn't make sense, or just kept confirming over and over what I wanted so much not to find, but could no longer deny—that the same kind of terribly destructive pseudospiritual politicking I had recently been exposed to had been going on in the Church since the nineteenth century. I wanted to let go of all my questions and let the Spirit fill me and lift me as it had done so often before in this sacred place, this historic building where the same men whose journals I'd studied had spoken publicly to the saints of their own day.

The Mormon Tabernacle Choir began to sing. "I Need Thee Every Hour." But there was no peace this time in those full vibrations of harmonic sound. Why did my Church work have to get in the way of my spirituality? Why couldn't the two be bound together the way they'd been for me before? Why couldn't things make sense?

President Tanner stood and began the proposals, the business portion of the Conference. There was the normal sustaining of the General Authorities and officers of the Church. Then he announced:

It is proposed that we sustain certain "Excerpts From Three Addresses by President Wilford Woodruff Regarding the Manifesto" and accept them as part of the Doctrine and Covenants and, therefore, binding upon the membership of the Church. All in favor, may manifest it by the raise of the right hand.

I had never before in my life voted not to sustain. But I couldn't believe what I'd heard him say. What was happening to the Church I loved? What was happening to the institution I'd devoted my life and career to? Did all these other people in the Tabernacle even know what they were voting on? Had they studied these three talks by Wilford Woodruff as I had?

In one of the addresses, he'd said: *The Lord will never permit me or any other man who stands as President of this*

Church to lead you astray. It is not in the programme. It is not the mind of God. Doctrine and Covenants, 1981 edition.

For a moment it seemed as if eternity stood still. I was separate from the thousands of saints assembled in the Tabernacle. It seemed I could look down on all of them as if from some great distance. I could see them, far below me, as they continued automatically to raise their right hands sustaining each proposal that was given to them by President Tanner. I saw myself as well, utterly apart and alone in my place on the Tabernacle bench. I had been a part of them; now I was being torn from them.

I didn't raise my hand. It was simply inconceivable that the leaders would not realize what these statements of President Woodruff had implied. Even the Roman Catholic popes had never claimed this kind of infallibility.

I sat there stunned. I couldn't help but think about Moses Thatcher, an Apostle during the time Wilford Woodruff was President of the Church. He was out of union with the rest of The Brethren. In fact, serious divisions existed among the Twelve and others of the leadership of the Church on many questions of doctrine and procedure. This division was so deep that Heber J. Grant recorded in his journal that he was ashamed of his own actions during that period. Wilford Woodruff also lamented in his journal over the extreme disunity that then existed in his quorum. The Twelve were evenly divided on nearly every issue on which they tried to make a decision.

During the time I'd spent pouring over microfilms and other materials in the Church archives, I'd seen that many of the leaders of the Church who'd worked with Wilford Woodruff had been strongly opposed to this particular statement of his—this statement that our Church had just accepted as scripture. Many even had felt that he was starting to lead the Church astray then because of his implied infallibility. In order to get a unanimous vote from the Council of the Twelve, Wilford Woodruff finally had to have Moses Thatcher "dropped" from his position in The Quorum.

Into the Church Archives

Why had the Church come to publicly elevate a statement such as this to the status of scripture, a statement that was so poorly received when it was originally presented? Had we changed that much, as a people?

I had seen in my research in the Church Historian's office that after the Manifesto of 1890 by Wilford Woodruff, there followed a series of decades in which a systematic reconstruction of Mormon doctrine took place. It was almost as if, with the taking away of an ability to practice the theological truths given by Joseph Smith, the principles that were the foundation to those practices had to be taken away also. I had reasoned that, perhaps, it was an effort to keep the saints from understanding the theology that leads to the practices which were being abandoned.

In 1890, Wilford Woodruff announced that plural marriage was no longer acceptable sacramental practice in the Church. In 1894, he stopped the practice of sealing men to men saying that "additional revelation" was necessary on the ordinance before it could be continued. Women were no longer referred to as "high priestesses," as had been a usual reference to women who ministered in temples. Eliza R. Snow had even been referred to as a prophetess and high priestess by some. And, there were more changes, many more that only served to confuse me.

Perhaps that was when I first knew that I could not in good conscience commit myself to this organization any longer. As much as I didn't want to, I knew that I needed to find another job and seek to be released from my position as Bishop. I couldn't be a hypocrite anymore. I didn't want to be double-minded. I could no longer trust the public wisdom of leaders who weren't producing "good fruit" in their private ecclesiastical endeavors. Truth had to be more important than "following the Brethren." I had been reminded over and over again by President Farnsworth that the perspective of the Church was exactly the opposite. "Remember, Bishop" he'd say to me, "the President is right, even when he's wrong. Your call is to obey and you will be blessed for your implicit obedience". How could any thinking person believe that?

In the days and weeks that followed, I realized all the more that one's spirituality is a personal, private communion. I had gained some spirituality within the context of the institutional Church, but I knew now that staying within that context would only harm my spiritual self. I had learned that the ordinances, especially those of the The Lord's House, taught the language of our God. However, each of us, individually and alone, still had to climb his or her own spiritual mountains.

This pronouncement of Wilford Woodruff, now accepted as holy scripture by the Mormon Church, put the Church above the individual saint. it put the President between the believer and The Father. By condemning them to an eternity of being followers, it denied members of the Church their divinely given right to seek true spirituality. Obedience was the first law of heaven, yes...but it was the first step at the bottom of the path leading upward. It's not an iron hand at the very top of a church structure which claimed to be completely infallible and requiring total acquiescence to its edicts.

I'd been up on the mountain of sublime spirituality. I knew the love of God. And I knew I'd be there again. But I also knew if I stayed where I was much longer, the Church would smother me. I wasn't willing to let that happen. I knew too much. As I'd studied and searched, as I'd worked closely with Church leaders at Church headquarters, and as I'd sought personally for the further light and knowledge which God had promised to us all, I'd experienced more than my wildest dreams could have hinted at. I knew I simply could not allow the Church's inadequacies to interfere with what I'd been given.

But, what about my family, my children? What would happen to our sealed union? As I pondered this question, I became convinced that staying in the Church would only hurt all of us, especially the children. I didn't want them to see their father living the life of a double-minded hypocrite. It would be better for them to believe their father was horribly mistaken and deceived than to have them witness an example of utter hypocrisy.

92

Into the Church Archives

My request for a release as the Bishop of our Ward was soon granted and once again I was called to teach the Gospel Doctrine class. It was harder to leave my employment at Church headquarters. I had worked in the Church Offices for almost six years, and loved my assignment in Welfare Services as Coordinator of Adult Education and Training for the Welfare Services Missionaries.

Shortly after that eventful Conference session, Laura and I prepared to attend one of the special banquets we had always held for the missionaries.

I knew as the group of missionaries left the training center, painful as it was for me to face, that this would be the last time I'd share this wonderful experience with my co-workers and a group of faithful missionaries. These were people who had committed their lives to the sharing of the gospel in an action-oriented manner. These were not the common rank and file of Mormon missionaries; these were Welfare Services Missionaries—faithful saints sent out to help raise the spiritual and temporal consciousness of others, not solely to convert them to the Church.

It was October 10, 1980, the anniversary of the death of our firstborn son. He would have been eleven, I thought to myself, as the piano played the prelude to the first musical number. I looked around our group assembled in the banquet room on the 26th floor of the Church Office Building.

Three of our instructors had prepared the evening's entertainment. They sang so beautifully. Stan started with a solo rendition, his voice melodious and clear...

As I have loved you, love one another.
This new commandment: Love one another.
By this shall men know ye are my disciples,
If ye love one another.

Then Rachel took the limelight with a solo interpretation of one of my favorite hymns: *"Love At Home."* When she was through, Jim brought my emotions to the surface with a marvelous rendition of a favorite hymn of Joseph Smith, the hymn he'd asked John Taylor to sing for him just before he'd been killed by a mob...

Out of the Bishop's Closet

A poor, wayfaring man of grief hath often
crossed me on my way;
Who sued so humbly for relief that
I chould never answer nay.

Then, all three of them joined in a blended chorus of these three different songs. It was a marvelous harmonious message that was unmistakable to me. My emotions responded to this call. This was a message to acquire love in all its dimensions of expression: Love for our fellows, love for our families, and love for strangers.

Laura nudged me gently and gave me a strange look when she saw I couldn't hold back my tears. I took the tissue she offered and dried my face. Joseph Smith had loved, truly loved. Why did there have to be such a lack of that love in the Church now? I'd spent days alone in my study since General Converence; I'd fasted and prayed for divine guidance on what I should do, wanting to be sure that leaving Church employment was the right choice. The tears kept coming.

"And now," Stan said, "we would like to sing a favorite of ours. It reflects the principles which we instructors endeavor to teach the missionaries at the Missionary Training Center. We felt very impressed to sing it here. It's an old Shaker folk song about 'turning' till we come out right."

"They've learned well what we've tried to teach them." I whispered to Laura. I was overcome with emotion at the thought of leaving these loving companions in the work of God. I would miss them.

Stan, Rachel, and Jim stood and sang one of the most beautiful, harmonic messages I've ever heard. It was the very message I needed to hear that night. Again, God was speaking to me through their music...

'Tis the gift to be simple—
'Tis the gift to be free—
'Tis the gift to come down where we ought to be.
And when we find ourselves in the place that's right,
It will be in the valley of love and delight!

'Tis the gift to be gentle—
'Tis the gift to be fair—
'Tis the gift to wake and breathe the morning air;
And every day to walk in the path that we choose;
'Tis the gift that we pray we may ne' er come to lose!

'Tis the gift to be loving—
'Tis the best gift of all;
Like a quiet rain, it blesses where it falls.
And if we have the gift, then we'll truly believe:
'Tis better to give than it is to receive!

When true simplicity is gained,
To bow and to bend, we shant be ashamed.
To turn, turn will be our delight,
'Till by turning, turning, we come out right!

The lyrics kept ringing over and over again in my ears, "To bow and to bend, we shan't be ashamed / To turn, turn will be our delight / Till by turning, turning we come out right." This was my answer. My confirmation had come through these beautiful, young dedicated colleagues of mine in their giftedness of musical skill. In the midst of my terrible confusion over the contradictions and dichotomies which, when researched, led me to even greater questions, here was direction. I felt that it would be very difficult but, I had no idea how difficult it would be to make the break from the Church I'd loved. Nevertheless, at that moment, I knew exactly what to do. The direction was clear and precise. Now it was my turn to experience my own "turning, turning" till I came out right.

I turned to look at Laura. As I saw her blur through the tears in my eyes, I knew I would miss her more than anything or anyone else.

When I heard at the close of the day how my name had
been receiv'd with plaudits in the capitol, still
it was not a happy night for me that follow'd
And else when I carous'd, or when my plans were
accomplish'd still I was not happy,
But the day when I rose at dawn from the bed of
perfect health refresh'd, singing, inhaling the
ripe of autumn,
When I saw the full moon in the west grow pale and
disappear in the morning light,
When I wander'd alone over the beach, and undressing
bathed laughing with the cool waters, and saw the
sun rise,
And when I thought how my dear friend my lover was
on his way coming, O then I was happy,
O then each breath tasted sweeter, and all that day
my food nourishe'd me more, and the beautiful day
pass'd well,
And the next came with equal joy, and with the next
at evening came my friend,
And that night while all was still I heard the
waters roll slowly continually up the shores,
I heard the hissing rustle of the liquid and sands
as directed to me whispering to congratulate me,
For the one I love most lay sleeping by me under
same cover in the cool night,
In the stillness in the autumn moonbeams his face
was inclined toward me,
And his arm lay lightly around my breast--and that
night I was happy.

Walt Whitman, "When I Heard At The Close Of The Day"
 Leaves of Grass
Published in Illinois, 1860

Chapter 6
Coming Out of The
Bishop's Closet

Burt was doing research in the archives of the Church when he called my office to let me know that he'd discovered something I would have an interest in. He knew that I'd been researching the person referred to by Joseph Smith as the "very friend" of Lorenzo Barnes in his funeral sermon of April 16, 1843. "It's in Wilford Woodruff's personal journal and President Woodruff appears to call this person the 'Lover' of Lorenzo Barnes."

"You're joking".

"Come see for yourself. He actually used the word 'Lover.'"

I was trying to catch a plane to California on an assignment in Sacramento, but I would stop everything for this. "I'll come right down to your floor." After hanging up the telephone, I did everything that was necessary so that I wouldn't have to return to my office afterward. I didn't want to jeopardize any time I'd need to fully examine this new find Burt had called me about.

We both sat there, in the thrill of a mutual discovery, reading the entry made by Wilford Woodruff dated February 20, 1845. The Apostle had gone to England and had visited the grave of the late Elder Lorenzo D. Barnes, the first Mormon missionary to die on a mission "in a foreign land."

As I stood upon his grave I realized I was standing over the body of one of the Elders of Israel...One whose fidelity was stronger than death towards his Lover, his brethren, eternal truth, & his God...I thought of his [-] Lover, his Mother, his Father, his kindred & the Saints for they all loved him...O Lorenzo thou hast fallen...But if thy God permits me to tread again the Courts of His house, in Zions land, & have access to the sealing powers, endowments, & keys of the kingdom of God I' ll remember thee & pray that thy exaltation may not be short of the Chiefest of thy quorums. Wilford Woodruff Journal, February 1845, pages 510-511

What was that shorthand-like figure before the word "Lover"? It looked like the drawing of a key, "What's that key-like drawing, Burt? Is it some kind of code?"

"Oh yes, Tony. Wilford Woodruff used to draw codes into his journals when he'd record things that he didn't feel should be talked about. Usually, when he'd use this key symbol, it represented things relative to 'priesthood' or 'sealings' or even 'the Kingdom of God' itself. It symbolized priesthood sealing keys or, at least, we think it did."

"So, in this case, do you think the key stood for Lorenzo Barnes' 'kingdom' Lover or 'priesthood' Lover or maybe for 'sealed' Lover?"

"Oh, there's no doubt at all in my mind about that."

I was astounded. Burt didn't know why I was so interested in this particular person. I knew I had to be very careful about what I said. I tried to contain myself. "Wow! those brethren sure seemed to have a different perspective than we do now."

"Oh yes, Tony. To them, the revelation on polygamy did much to liberalize the cultural norms of their day. Also, marriage as an institution was not so much a civil act as it was religious."

"Do you have any idea who this person Wilford Woodruff was writing about here as the 'Lover' of Lorenzo Barnes?"

"No. But, we'll just have to continue the research."

"Thanks Burt. I have to run. I'm due out at the airport to catch a plane to California." I was torn. I wanted to stay.

Coming Out of the Bishop's Closet

"You guys in Welfare Services get all the perky assignments, don't you?" He laughed.

With that, I left his office. But, the scene of looking into that microfilm screen was still too vivid for me to think of anything else. Wilford Woodruff had actually called the person whom Lorenzo Barnes had been faithful to as the "Lover" of Lorenzo Barnes—not his spouse, wife, companion, intended, or even his fiancé. He'd called that person Lorenzo Barnes' "Lover"! I remembered reading the poems of Walt Whitman in his *Leaves of Grass,* and how I'd been shocked with his use of the word "lover" as a reference to his male friend. I'd remembered that Walt Whitman had lived close to Nauvoo, Illinois and that this particular poem had been written by him about the same time that Wilford Woodruff and Joseph and the others lived there. I reasoned that surely the use of the word "Lover" by Wilford Woodruff must have been in the same context as the way Walt Whitman had used it. I thought of little else on the flight.

After getting off the plane, my efforts were geared to get my work done as quickly as possible. I had the meetings I'd set up with the local Welfare Services employees of the Church scheduled in their various places of work. I couldn't get them finished fast enough. I had planned to get the work done as early as possible for a reason, a reason I hadn't shared with anyone else...

The voice on the telephone said, "Club Baths* of Sacramento. This is Dale; may I help you?" I was shaking as if I had a fever. I could hardly hold the phone. I knew that if I tried to speak, my voice would certainly start shaking as much as the rest of me was. I almost hung up without speaking, then finally blurted out, "I'm in town on business and I've never had sex with a man and I'm scared!"

---

*This experience took place before AIDS. While I saw gay bath houses as evil, I knew of no other place to meet others.

Out of the Bishop's Closet

It was Wednesday afternoon. I had finished my meetings and other work. I called home to tell Laura I wouldn't be back until Sunday. She seemed to sense I needed time to be alone. It almost seemed too easy to get the time off from work. I was alone in a strange city where no one knew me.

Before my previous trip to California, I'd never heard of such a thing as a gay bathhouse. But on my trip to meet with the manager of the Employment Center in San Jose, I'd discovered a copy of *The Advocate* that had been left in the trunk of the car I'd rented.

As I stood there in the telephone booth in Sacramento, I recalled the exact position in the middle of the right side of the right page where all the Club Baths had been advertised. I'd read that paper avidly. I had found it provocative and erotic and informative all at once. And then, of course, I immediately disposed of it. But the telephone number I'd just dialed had been echoing through my mind for weeks. I couldn't have forgotten those seven numbers even if I'd wanted to.

"Why don't you come and see us?" Dale invited. "I'll give you a tour, and if you don't want to stay, that's fine." He had such a soothing, sweet, and calming sound to his voice. He made me feel that I didn't need to be afraid. He didn't know me. Nobody knew me. I was still safely anonymous in the phone booth. Nobody was going to find me out. If I just hung up now and went back to my hotel room, no one would ever even know I'd actually called a gay bathhouse. I could go back right now. But to what? Back to my frustrations. Back to my loneliness. Back to my lies about myself. Back to trying to be something I wasn't? Back to living life as somebody else instead of as myself as I probably was in my heart of hearts?

I leaned against the side of the telephone booth to steady myself, and switched the receiver to my other hand. It was a little less sweaty, but not much. "Okay," I said, "I will."

He asked my name.

I hesitated. "Tony," I said finally. "My name's Tony."

Coming Out of the Bishop's Closet

I had made a commitment to myself years before that I would never act on my homosexual desires, no matter how strong they might become. I believed that homosexuality was a sin. The leaders whom I revered as Prophets of God had taught me that what I was and what I felt was evil and ugly and unnatural, and I'd believed them. But I just couldn't believe them any more.

I pulled up in front of the bathhouse and parked the car. A few minutes later, I waited in line while a man in front of me dressed in leather clothing signed his name and paid his fee prior to entering the place. It was dark inside, obviously in a state of remodeling. I wondered what better light would reveal.

Finally my turn came. "You must be Tony," the young man behind the window said with a glowing smile.

"How did you know?" I asked in confusion.

He laughed. "It's not everyone who comes to a gay bathhouse dressed in clothes like that."

I glanced down at what I had on. I hadn't stopped to think that my navy blue business suit, white shirt and burgandy tie might be unusual attire for the place I'd come to visit.

Dale could see my sudden embarrassment. He buzzed the door. "Come on in."

I pushed the door open.

"Hey, I won't bite," he said, still smiling. "You're okay. You ready for the tour?"

"As ready as I'll ever be, I guess," I said. Dale was a young man in his late twenties or early thirties about five feet ten and with almost glowing, clear eyes that radiated warmth. His smile was beautiful and healthy, and was accentuated by the fullness of his dark hair which had been cut short to his ears. He was clean looking and poised in his manner. I found myself watching his body move as he turned around and began to walk away. I wondered if he worked out.

He led me down the steps to a dim hallway. I'd started to shake again. What was I doing here anyway? Wasn't this

101

the kind of place that all the Prophets had warned about? Wasn't this certainly one of the "dens of iniquity" I'd been taught about in Sunday School class?

But somehow it didn't feel evil. It just felt new, somehow, like being alone on the first day of school or my first taste of chocolate at seven. I was seeing something I'd never seen before. Glimpses of a new world opened in front of me.

Wednesday afternoons were not an especially busy time at the club; business was slow. Dale and I walked relatively alone in the darkness-filled alcoves and hallways. He led me past rooms set up for video-watching, and games, and other activities—the substance of which I could only imagine. As we passed by the common showers and the rooms where pornographic movies were being shown on the television screen, I realized again how ridiculous I must look in the conservative "bishop's suit" that I always wore on official Church business. But there was nothing I could do about it now.

I stopped for a moment to look into one room. When I turned back, I couldn't see where Dale had gone. There was a faint light from the cross hallway where I thought we'd turned, but I hadn't really been paying attention to the maze of rooms and halls. I'd just followed him. But where was he? How could he leave me alone like this in a place I didn't know? I turned in confusion in the near darkness, wondering which way to go.

All of a sudden I was in ecstasy. I was being kissed by another man.

When he finally spoke, I instantly recognized his voice. It was that same soothing, sweet, calm voice I'd heard for the first time when I'd stood shaking in the telephone booth earlier that day.

"These are directions to my place," Dale said quietly. "The key's wrapped inside. I get off work in three hours. Make yourself at home and wait for me there."

102

Coming Out of the Bishop's Closet

"I'd love to." The words were out of my mouth before I even knew I'd said them. Why did I trust him so much? How could he trust me, a total stranger?

He kissed me again, holding me close, his arms around me. For some reason I felt totally safe in his arms. Complete and secure.

As I left the buzzing door behind me, I turned back to him once again. "You're sure this is all right?"

He grinned in response. "Don't worry. Nobody's going to hurt you. You're okay, remember?"

I got into the car and looked at the directions he'd given me. I was about to find out who and what I really was. I wasn't going to fight it anymore. In Dale's arms in the dark hallway of the bathhouse I felt something I'd never felt before. I couldn't deny that what I felt was the real me.

I hesitantly let myself into Dale's home, feeling almost like an intruder. The feeling of newness I'd felt in the bathhouse came back with new intensity. The man who lived here enjoyed the kind of openly gay lifestyle that I could only fantasize about. I marveled at how tastefully the rooms were decorated. From the waterbed to the piano to the fashionable wall decor, they could almost have been lifted from a furniture store showroom.

I looked through the books on his shelves. He was a musician with tastes that mirrored my own. I picked up some of the sheet music on the piano. Gospel music had always been a favorite of mine too. I began to read some of the books he had that addressed gay/Christian, issues and was quickly and intensely rapt in complete fascination at the theology I was reading; it made logical sense and yet was all so new.

My mind was filled with questions.

When Dale arrived, I felt a little awkward letting him in. "Welcome to your home!" I said.

Then, as if nothing had taken place between us back at the bathhouse, he said, "What do you want to eat? I'm a pretty good cook."

"Can I ask you some questions about the stuff I've been reading in your library while you're getting things ready?"

He laughed and winked at me. "Sure, but only if you help with the dishes."

M. Dale Hansen told me he'd been very active as a member of a fundamentalist Christian church in Orange County, and that he'd been involved in Gospel singing professionally. As he talked, it was obvious that he loved the Lord. He'd made a personal decision that he shouldn't be involved with a church that didn't accept him as worthy, even though they knew nothing of his personal intimate life. He had voluntarily withdrawn from active participation in his music ministry.

"I had to take playing the hypocrite out of my life," he explained. "When Jesus was on the earth, the one thing he taught against more than any other sin was hypocrisy. Christ never said anything against homosexuality, but he said a lot about hypocrisy. I realized I couldn't choose not to be gay, but I could choose not to be a hypocrite."

"But what about what Paul wrote?" I asked as he set salads in front of us. "And the things Moses said?"

"Well, in the first place, much of what the New Testament translators gave us has been mistranslated and is definitely misinterpreted. If we were to take the statements attributed to Paul in the New Testament as evidence that homosexuality is wrong, then we'd also have to take literally his other remarks in those same chapters."

I tried to remember everything Paul had said.

"He said women shouldn't speak in church. He said women had to wear hats in church. He said gold should not be allowed to be worn in church. If you remember, he gave some pretty strong warnings against marriage."

104

What he said made sense. I'd never heard things explained from this perspective. Over dessert, I learned Dale's views on the Levitical prohibitions outlined in the Old Testament. "That law is no longer in force," he reminded me. "It was fulfilled in Christ."

"What about Sodom and Gomorrah?"

He reached for his Bible, and began to read the story to me, giving me a verse-by-verse commentary. As he shed more and more light on this story, I kept remembering what Nephi had predicted about the Bible as he painstakingly engraved the record that would become the *Book of Mormon*:

Wherefore, these things (the Bible) go forth from the Jews in purity unto the Gentiles, according to truth which is in God.

And after they go forth by the hand of the twelve apostles of the Lamb, from the Jews unto the Gentiles, thou seest...they have taken away from the gospel of the Lamb many parts which are plain and most precious; and also many covenants of the Lord have they taken away.

And all this have they done that they might pervert the right ways of the Lord, that they might blind the eyes and harden the hearts of the children of men. (I Nephi 13:25-27)

Dale read the first three verses of Genesis chapter 19. "You see, Tony," he explained. "These angels were traveling in a desert plain and the rule of society in those days in that area was that you were hospitable to travelers. That's what Lot was trying to offer—his hospitality. He was a good man. You'll remember that earlier Abraham had gotten a promise from God that He would spare the city if there were at least ten good men in it. Lot was one."

He read verse 4. "You know these 'men of the city' weren't representative of gay men because the scripture makes it clear that these 'men of Sodom' were 'all the people from every quarter.' Tony, this was everyone, not just the gay population."

105

"But look at this," I said, pointing to verse 5. "Doesn't the wording, 'bring them out unto us, that we may know them' mean that they wanted to 'know' these angels sexually?"

"Not really. The Hebrew word used in this verse is YADHA. YADHA is the same term used by Jesus when he said, 'To know me is to know God.' It's used 943 times in the Old and New Testaments. It's used two times in heterosexual connotations. Ten times its use is not clear, and the other 931 uses are all totally nonsexual. The people in ancient Sodom simply wanted to know these people who were visiting Lot. To say their motives were purely sexual and specifically homosexual is totally unfounded, even though that's what's usually taught."

"Okay. But, what about the fact that Moses uses the word 'abomination' in reference to the acts that these people were doing and in Leviticus when he wrote that for a man to lie with another man was 'abomination' in the eyes of God?"

"Abomination, Tony, is the word that's been translated from that which was ritually or ceremonially 'unclean' to ancient Hebrews. It wasn't intrinsically evil. To them there was a prohibition to mimic pagans because that would be almost like worshiping the pagan gods and pagans would practice both heterosexual and homosexual love making in their pagan temples."

We cleared the table and washed the dishes together. We learned we both had a deep and abiding commitment to God and to the Christian ethic. For both of us, this was more important than anything else in our lives. He had been raised in a strong Christian home, just as I had been.

"You've taught me so much, Dale." We were sprawled comfortably on the couch next to each other, my knee just barely touching his. "Thanks."

He laughed easily, as if it had not really been that much. "I have a lot more than that to teach you, Tony." It was not a statement. It was an invitation. He put his hand on my leg, drawing invisible circles with his fingertips. "Are you ready to learn?"

Coming Out of the Bishop's Closet

"I...I don't know."

Why had I come here if not for this? Who was I kidding? But how was I going to feel afterwards? I didn't care how I'd feel. I wanted him to kiss me again. I wanted to kiss him back. I wanted to share what I felt inside with someone who felt the same way, to give expression to the wordless ache for wholeness that gripped my insides and would not let me go.

"Look, Tony, it's okay to be gay. You're gay. Let your whole self be gay. Don't fight it anymore." His voice dropped to almost a whisper. "You don't have to fight it here."

I wanted to give in. I wanted to relinquish myself to him. I wanted to let go of all the lies I'd believed all my life, all the painful fictions I'd accepted as God's truth. I wanted him to take them from me, to set me free. But I'd held on to them so tightly for so long. I couldn't let go.

He slid his hand under the collar of my shirt. A tremor shook me. He touched my neck with the lightest of caresses, then gently turned my face towards his. He looked into my eyes for a minute as if perhaps the secret to my fear was hidden there. Then he smiled again, that easy smile, already so familiar, that made me love him, and shook his head, laughing a little as if he almost couldn't believe a person like me actually existed.

"What are you afraid of? I won't hurt you." And then, as if to prove this, he pulled me off the couch onto the carpet and, pinning me beneath him, began to kiss me again with the same fierce intensity he'd shown earlier that day. Something broke inside me. I couldn't hold back anymore. I returned his kisses. He loved me. I loved him. Passionately. Thoroughly. Intimately.

I learned finally what it really was I had always wanted. I learned what it was I needed. I learned what it was I loved in love making. Dale had been right. He did have much to teach me. And, in those moments afterward, I was sure he'd been sent by God to me—a hand picked trainer from God, himself—just for me.

"Well?" he whispered as we lay together afterwards, satisfied and sleepy and spent, "Tell me now, Bishop Tony Feliz, how do you like being gay?"

It was the word "Bishop" that did it. I was a Bishop! What in God's name was I doing here, making love with a... with a man? How could I have done this to Laura? What was wrong with me anyway? Disgust for myself and my body darkened the joy I'd felt in Dale's touch just a moment before. Revulsion writhed through me, overpowering and awful. I wanted to be out of myself. I wanted to be anyone but me.

Dale was patient as I attacked myself. "You pour your own guilt on yourself like water out of a shower nozzle," he said. "It's as if you think that if you pour enough guilt on yourself, you'll be clean. You're clean already. You don't have to feel guilty for being yourself." He took me into his arms again. Thoughts of guilt dissolved into passion.

Those first few hours together turned into four beautiful days and nights of profound conversation and intimacy. We talked, we ate, we loved, we talked some more. In the midst of passion and emotion, our spirit-selves blended and meshed like nothing I had ever experienced before. I was convinced that no one else on the entire planet could make love to me like this man. No one.

But then, when our bodies, as instruments of such intimate, intense communication became relaxed, my mind came sneaking back with all its old worn-out accusations. I felt awful and hated myself; then Dale would take me and make me whole once more. He showed me parts of myself I'd never known, opened whole new vistas of myself to me. He knew exactly what I needed in order to understand my whole being.

By the third day, I felt he knew more about me than maybe anyone else in the world. It amazed me that, knowing that much about me, he would still want to know me and would still want to love me as he said he did.

"What you need to realize, Tony," he said one morning as the sun streaked through the window of his bedroom, "is that God loves gay people too. Do you believe that?"

Coming Out of the Bishop's Closet

I wanted to believe it. I wanted to believe God loved me. But, it wasn't that easy. I'd believed for so long that God loved everyone, yes...but God, I'd been taught, expected more of me and other Mormons than He did of anybody else. I wanted to believe Dale. I wanted him to touch me, to not have this feeling of love and caring for each other stop. I had never felt this way before and I knew why. It was because I'd never been with a man before. And here was a man who both understood gay sexuality and understood the reality of what love between any two human beings could be, irrespective of either's gender.

For the first time in my life, I allowed myself to think about what I liked in sexual intimacy, what I felt natural doing sexually with another person. I'd never let myself do this before. I'd never before experienced such total relinquishment, such complete submission interwoven with another man's response. I'd never before known what my natural response would be to the intimate trust another man would place in me as I returned his love making. Hadn't the Church taught that "all desires, appetites, and passions" were to be kept within the bounds the Lord had set?

"But God didn't make all those rules, Tony." Dale begged me to open my mind. "You have to decode what God's said for yourself. You have to figure out what he really means. You can't depend on any church to do that for you. That's what the Holy Spirit is for."

For so long, God and the Church had been inseparable. God worked through the Church. The Church was supposed to be the Kingdom of God on earth. It seemed that if I started interpreting God's word for myself, it'd be easy to rationalize my way into believing anything I wanted to. I'd known so many people who'd rationalized their sins away only to still have the guilt when they finally came to their senses. I didn't want to fall into that trap.

"But you know if you're rationalizing or not," Dale argued. "Look inside yourself and accept what you see there.

God made you, Tony, and He didn't make a mistake. You've got to know that, deep within you."

I'd been looking outside of myself for guidance so long, accepting what others said I should be and feel, and punishing myself because I couldn't be the person they thought I should be.

"What do you think 'coming out' really means?" Dale asked me Saturday night. We both knew our time together was fast coming to an end.

"Not being afraid to let other people know I'm gay?"

"Partly. But there's more to it than that."

I wasn't sure what he meant.

"The most important part of coming out is for you to accept the fact that you're gay. For you to stop hating yourself because you're gay. You're good, Tony."

When he held me and we made love, I knew it. When we stopped, I felt awful again. I was like a newborn child. I hadn't developed any life-support systems outside of my "bishop's closet." I found comfort with Dale, who understood, almost instinctively, what my needs were—very much like a mother who nourishes and nurtures her newly born infant. But when the "feeding time" was over, it wasn't long before I hurt again, ignorant of how to deal with my new surroundings. Like a new baby, I was surrounded by new sensations—feelings of warmth and satisfaction and love, but also feelings of pain, discomfort, and hurt. I'd been in a womb of ignorance, protected by my lack of experience. Now I was going to experience the whole of life.

And as pertaining to the new and everlasting covenant, It was instituted for the fulness of my glory...

And verily I say unto you, that the conditions of this law are these; All covenants, contracts, bonds obligations oaths, vows, performances, connections, associations, or expectations...

And again, verily I say unto you, my servant Joseph, that whatsoever you give on earth, and to whomsoever you give any one on earth, by my word and according to my law, it shall be visited with blessings and not cursings, and with my power, saith the Lord, and shall be without condemnation on earth and in heaven.

Revelation given through Joseph Smith
at Nauvoo, Illinois, recorded July 12, 1843
Doctrine and Covenants (L.D.S.) Section 132: 6, 7, 48

Chapter 7
The Clouds of Separation

There is perhaps a part of all of us that is afraid to say to another person, "I love you,"unless we are already quite sure that the other knows of our love and accepts it. Love is a gift, and it's a gift that is sometimes difficult for us to give unless we're confident beforehand of how it will be received. It may be that this was the same hesitation that kept me from saying to Laura, "I'm gay," until I was sure her response would be, "I know."

I wanted her to see it for herself. I needed her to tell me it was all right, that she could accept me even with all my weaknesses and questions, even being gay. But I saw I'd asked too much of her. I didn't want her to say that I should continue on with gay relationships outside our marriage. That was not what I had in mind. I wanted acceptance, just simple acknowledgment that I was gay and that it was okay to her that I was gay. Then, I had reasoned, we could talk openly and together we'd get answers. We had always considered ourselves each other's "best friend" and the fourteen years of our marriage reflected that kind of union. I wanted to keep that. Of all things, I needed to keep that.

I simply couldn't face it alone anymore. I had to allow her to be part of this dilemma with me. In reality, she already was as my wife. Right now, though, I needed my "best friend."

I stopped being intimate with her in bed. "This will communicate where my words can't," I thought.

113

When we talked of homosexuality in general terms, her response was always one of horror. She had a cousin whose husband had told her he was gay. Whenever Laura spoke of it, it was obvious that homosexuality was one of the worst things she could imagine.

My theological dilemmas continued. Laura struggled to understand the frustrating contradictions I saw in Mormonism and I increased my efforts to share with her. "We're a 'forever' family, Tony. We're sealed for eternity," she'd plead, begging me not to doubt, asking me to stop questioning. She wanted the old Tony back, the man who had warned her to "love and obey God above me, Laura!" She wanted a man with a faith to match hers. Laura was not going to change from where we'd both begun.

I had changed, however. I no longer knew if I was willing to sacrifice everything unquestioningly for the Kingdom of God. I did know, however, that I was certainly not willing anymore to make a great sacrifice for the Church! The real question was: Was I willing to sacrifice for our marriage, to keep our family together? As a Bishop and as a High Councilor in the Church, I'd heard of many other couples who had decided on divorce because one in the union had left the Church. I'd told Laura, "In the same dilemma, I would choose God. Your choice, Laura, should be no different. It would be better for you to leave me than to leave God." But I couldn't be that man anymore. I wasn't that same man. So, if it now came to a choice for her between her husband and her God, I knew she would choose her God. As it had once been for me, her God was still "perfectly" embodied in her Church.

She wouldn't choose her "best friend."

I had been teaching Gospel Doctrine Class for several months and Laura kept complaining that my theological differences were showing up in the lessons every Sunday. So when I was offered a job with Hughes Aircraft Company in El Segundo, California, I took it so that I could get away from the environment of a Mormon community. I tried to convince Laura it would be best for her and the children to stay in Salt Lake City while I went on alone to California. I felt that perhaps, through this separation, she would be able to see the reality of where our marriage was headed. To me, the pain on the horizon was far too visible. One of us had to serve as guide through the rough road ahead.

She agreed to stay temporarily, at least until the house was sold. We talked to an attorney about the possibility of a divorce, but no final decisions were made. Laura was, above all else, a Latter-day Saint. I couldn't fault her for her total commitment to the Church and its teachings because that's exactly where my mind-set had been only a few years before. This was, in fact, one of the things that had attracted me to her in the first place. The Church taught women to sustain their husbands, to follow them, obey them, and support them as they led their families in righteousness. Laura wanted to do this. This was her reason for being. She wanted us to be one, to be united in our beliefs and desires, to share the same visions of what life was and what it could be. It's how our lives had been for almost fourteen years, and she wanted it to continue. However, the more I questioned and the closer I came to realizing I could no longer align myself with the Church as it had become, the more difficult things were for us. Even without considering my coming out, if we were to have our marriage return back to the welded kind of a marriage we had been, she would have had to change her views on the Church as I had. My theological dilemas had pulled me apart. In my new spiritual walk, I wouldn't turn back. I couldn't turn back.

Laura, I think, may have felt she was being pulled apart in another way: Laura's lifelong commitment to the Church pulled her in one direction; her earnest desire to stay with me, once such an integral part of her devotion to her Church, now pulled her in another; and our children—our eager, trusting, vulnerable children who were now getting old enough to ask difficult questions—pulled her in yet another. What was best for them? How could she answer them? How would their emotional, spiritual, and social lives be affected by all this?

My grandmother, who was living with us at the time, had smoked cigarettes since her fifth birthday. She was ninety-eight and her existence defied all the rhetoric our children had heard, Church Primary teachers notwithstanding. "Is Gramma a bad person?" little Joseph would ask with Rafael standing by, also listening to hear what our answer would be. "Does God not like her because she smokes and drinks coffee?"

Somehow, I could always hear another question in that innocent wondering of his, a question he might never be able to ask aloud, but would wrestle with nonetheless. "Is Dad a bad person? Does God not love Dad because he's gay?" Was it any different? Laura wanted to teach the children that absolutes exist, that laws are set forth by God to be obeyed, that strict adherence to the tenets of Mormonism was the only way to be exalted. It was what I had once wanted as well. I'd held these small, innocent, believing children on my lap as we gathered in our Family Home Evening and I had told them over and over again that ours was the only true church. But, now there was so much *more* I wanted them to know. I wanted to teach them to love, to love themselves and those around them, to be open to truth from every source, to be honest with themselves, to be accepting of others in their differences. They were the generation who could bring about Zion, and now I knew what they needed to know in order to make that happen. But, in my perspective, what they needed to know had to be experienced both within and without the Church.

We attended church together the last Sunday before I was to leave for California. As the Fast and Testimony meeting began, I could not get God's first words to Joseph Smith out of my mind:

"Their hearts are far from me...and they teach for doctrine the commandments of men."

Had he known, Prophet that he was, that the Church would come to this? That the pure and boundless gospel he taught would be lost, as theories and dogma and human reasoning were mistaken for absolute truth revealed by God? Why, why had the membership of the Church allowed their theology to get so caught up in speculation and in limited ideas tied to only one culture? Why couldn't they see that eternal principles were just that — eternal? Eternal principles could not be restricted by the understanding of just one societal culture! The principles had to be adaptable to "every nation, kindred, tongue and people." Every people, even gay people.

We sang a hymn. The bread and water were blessed and passed to the members. I knew I must stand and bear testimony. I knew I must speak to the members of my Ward one last time.

I listened as others spoke, and then, when the meeting was nearly over, I walked to the stand. I looked out over the people I loved, the people who had shared their many-faceted lives with me. I'd been before them so many times before, pleading, exhorting, counseling. I'd believed we could become a Zion people. It had been my only goal. Had they heard me? Had any of them heard me? Had any of them understood what the word ZION means, what it represents? Had they understood that it wasn't just a place, that it was a condition of purity, clarity, and loving, harmonious union?

What could I say to help them see? How could I awaken them to what the Church—all of us—were letting happen? I couldn't think of anything other than the experience I'd had in General Conference. My mind was stuck on the "infallibility" statement which the Presidency of the Church had added to accepted scripture. I kept remembering the old records I'd seen in the archives at the Church Offices, how divided The Twelve had been on these very words which had been made scripture. A familiar passage of scripture screamed from inside me. I was filled with it. It could not be contained. I would speak to them with Moroni's words, not with my own. I was overcome by what must have been the same agonizing mantle he'd felt. I wasn't condemning but the message was there, clear and unequivocal, in the words that all of us accepted as God's word to the Church. These were words from an ancient Prophet to us, to this generation of the latter-day "people of God"—to today's Church.

I opened my *Book of Mormon* and read:

Behold, I speak unto you as if ye were present, and yet ye are not. But behold, Jesus Christ hath shown you unto me, and I know your doing...

...and your churches, yea, even every one, have become polluted because of the pride of your hearts...

...oh ye pollutions, ye hypocrites...why have ye polluted the holy church of God? Mormon 8:35,36,38

I closed the book and said, "In the Name of Christ, amen". I started to walk down the aisle toward my family. It's the leaders, I thought to myself. The leaders! Who else was in a position to stop the polutions that the *Book of Mormon* prophet had foreseen in "the *holy* church of God?". According to the doctrine, the Mormon Church is the only *true* church on the earth. It is, therefore, the only church that could be considered the "holy church of God" and only its leaders could qualifiy as leaders of the "holy church of God."

Laura was crying. I sat back down next to her. In my heart, I had not only left the Church; but in separating myself from the Church, I had gone from her as well. I did not know how to comfort her. For her, my leaving the Church was also leaving Mormonism. I had not yet made a decision on Mormonism, but the Church was no longer an organization I could remain a part of. To me, it had become something very different from the church Joseph Smith founded.

I went to California alone.

Dale's number in Sacramento had been disconnected. I called his mother in Montana. She said she wasn't sure when she would hear from him, but she would give him my message. He didn't call. I needed him. He'd opened a part of myself to me that I'd never known before and taught me to love it. I had to find him.

The Clouds of Separation

Dale had a birthmark near his shoulder that a doctor had told him would need to be surgically removed. I found myself asking everyone I met if they knew a "Dale Hansen" with such a mark. No one did. Had I driven him away by my constant guilt-ridden antics after our lovemaking? Had he finally wearied of my unending self-deprecation?

He'd been honest enough and loving enough and caring enough to show me by his own example that God loved me and cared for me just as I was. At the time I needed most to learn it, he had taught me that there were other ways to see life than the way I'd looked at it for so long. It was in his arms that I'd finally learned what we mean when we say, "God is love." If it had not been for him, I might never have been able to admit that I was gay; I might still be living a lie. But, *with him* I could imagine that one day I would be whole, and could then stop being "double-minded." I wanted to live with him, to share every part of my life with him. I wanted to stop being a hypocrite. If I was gay, I thought, I should still live as moral a life as possible, and that meant I had to be with Dale, there could be no one else. But I couldn't find him.

"Son," my mother asked me once during my first lonely days in southern California, "Tell me what it is about a man that could make you want him sexually in bed with you more than a woman?"

I tried to explain. "I love Laura," I told her, "in a way I've never loved anyone else. But, let me tell you about someone I've been with." I wanted her to understand what I felt when I was with Dale, to let her see why I would want to be with him more than anyone else in the world.

"At first," I said, "I was confused by what the Church taught me on the one hand, and what I knew was my own reality, on the other. I was so mixed up about everything that I couldn't make love to him. So, he made love to me and he showed me that it was okay for me to be the way I am. When

I'm with him, it's the most comfortable and emotionally warm feeling of my life."

She looked at me, shaking her head, still trying to understand.

"It's not just physical, Mom. It's a whole and complete sensation of security and rightness. When I feel his warm body next to mine, the affections of my heart have an object that they've never had before, allowing them to go full circle in a way I've never experienced." I thought of something that I might try to relate it to for her and said, "Since Dad died, isn't there a certain something missing now, from your life that needs to be brought back into your life in order for you to be whole again?"

"Well, you're a good man, Son," she sighed. "I don't understand this, but I can see you really do love this man. Maybe that's all I need to know. I hope you find yourself a good man that will be for you what you need to be for another."

When Bill and I met, I knew that he was exactly what I needed. I was new to Hollywood. I was lonely. I didn't have a ready-made family that I could go to like my local Mormon Ward. I didn't know how to meet other gay men. Bill was the personification of clean-cut, all-American, single, male health! He had a smile that would put toothpaste commercials to shame, a complexion that was luminesce with health. Most of all, Bill had spice! If I've ever met anyone who was alive in his life, instead of just living it, it was Bill Detton.

My work at Hughes was okay. When Bill suggested we become roommates, I was in heaven! To be roommates with a person who was always together, up, and active was just what I wanted. Soon our friends were coming over regularly for dinner; Bill was the best cook I'd ever experienced. His meals were always something out of a gourmet magazine or some fine place of palate pampering. At this juncture of my life, I had never even so much as tasted gourmet coffee or fine wine, not to speak of the many other scrumptious and sumptuous delicacies he saw to it that I experienced. If there is such a thing as a coming out to one's sensousness, this was it!

It was with Bill that I rediscovered how to laugh. I had never been to a gay bar before in my life, so...yes...to say the least, I was very nervous about the whole idea of going. Bill had planned the entire evening. It was going to be a blitz of the best that southern California's gay nightlife had to offer and was it ever! For the first time in my life, I actually saw men dancing with men. At one place, the men weren't even slow dancing, they weren't even swing dancing; these guys were doing the old dances I'd learned in my old Mormon Saturday-night folk-dance sessions! I loved to do the shuffle steps I'd learned in the old pioneer style that was now introduced to me as a "western shuffle"! But this time, almost twenty years later, I was able to live a fantasy: I did it with other men!

Life was good. It was Bill who said one day when we were both in the bathroom getting ready for another Saturday's fun: "Hey, Tony! Have you ever been high up in a hot-air balloon?" We both yelled out right there in anticipation at the thought. I realized that we'd screamed, deafening our ears as we yelled out! My joy in experiencing life at its heart's vitality was fantastic as several of us soared in those balloon rides during those months Bill and I lived together. I'd acquired a certain zest for life, and I had Bill to thank for it.

It was Bill who answered the front door when Laura knocked. I heard him say, "Just a minute. I'll get him." Even after she'd told me she was coming, I hadn't really thought she'd come and follow me to California.

"Tony," he hissed in a panic-stricken whisper, as he pressed me back into a corner of the room so she wouldn't hear. "It's your wife! What are you going to do?"

I shook my head helplessly, wanting him to tell me. Maybe at least, she'd finally see that I really was gay. Bill motioned toward the door and disappeared into the bathroom. I opened the door and let Laura into our one-room studio apartment. Silence hung awkwardly in the air as we both struggled with our unspoken emotions. Laura spoke first.

Out of the Bishop's Closet

"My place is here with you, Tony. We can make it work, if we both really want to."

I looked away from her in frustration. "Laura," I began, then stopped, still not knowing how to make her see, make her believe. Couldn't she see how I was living? Couldn't she see this tiny apartment with one bed?

The bathroom door opened. "Uh, look, guys," Bill said uncomfortably. "It looks as if you need to talk. I'm going out on a walk for a while." He left me alone with her.

"I can't make any promises, Laura," I said. "You know I can't promise I'll be faithful to you."

"I know you will be," she said stubbornly. "I know you can be, if you really want to."

"Does she finally know?" I wondered to myself. If she really did understand about my being gay, and still wanted us to get back together, then maybe it could work. Maybe I should try one more time.

But, I didn't really want to. I had learned too much about another Tony that Laura knew absolutely nothing about. How could I make her see that? There was no way I could without actually showing her. I was confused. I still loved Laura.

I suggested that Gregg Alda move in with Bill to help with the rent and Bill agreed. They'd be good roommates.

Laura, the children, and I moved into my mother's Ward and rented a home in Lake Elsinore, California, east of Los Angeles County. After registering the older children in school, our family returned to a semblance of "normalcy," We had committed ourselves to each other for eternity. It was not a covenant to be broken lightly, not a covenant either of us wanted to break. I think Laura needed to feel she'd done everything in her power to reconcile the differences between us before the painful decision to divorce was irreversibly made. I'd already accepted that outcome as I made the decision to leave Utah and the Church. Now, it was Laura's turn to fully decide. I would stay with her until she caught up with me in finding out more about the person she'd married. It seemed rational that if it took me so long to really approach understanding my true nature, she would take at least that long also.

Again, I was assigned by our Bishop to teach the Gospel Doctrine course on Sundays. I felt the Spirit strongly during those months as the instructor in that Ward. It was generally taught over the pulpit that people who are "living in sin" have no right to have the Spirit of God. But I knew I did. People from my class would comment to me on the inspired nature of my lessons during those months. I knew that it was because I was finally being honest with myself and with my God. I'd made my decision not to be a hypocrite anymore. Even though I'd never thought of myself as one, I had come to realize that in my suppression of my true gay nature, I had been a hypocrite. God knew I was gay and I sought His Spirit in my lesson preparations. As I did so, I could sense the Spirit blessing my lessons.

I dated other men. I didn't try to hide it from Laura. Although it seemed impossible, she still refused to believe that I was gay. Finally, I got her to go with me to see *Making Love,* a movie about the coming out of a gay medical doctor. It was during the scene when the gay doctor is trying to verbally explain his hidden desires to his wife that Laura finally could relate. A rigidness was reflected in her face from that point on until we began to talk in the privacy of our own bedroom. It was almost as if the movie were on and we were playing out the roles. Our own conversation that night seemed to be a reenactment of the scene in the movie. The children were all asleep, their doors were closed and the sitter had gone home. In our effort to keep our voices low but still communicate, the tension of our conversation created such energy that we found ourselves pacing from the bedroom into the living room and kitchen. We followed each other from one room to the other waving our hands with the emotion of our crisis. Our whispered talking soon became very loud.

123

She looked at me in disbelief. It was her place to sustain me, to support me, to love me. How could she accept this? She, who had always accepted whatever I'd said, who had willingly followed wherever I'd led. A Mormon woman was conditioned to be obedient to her husband. It was a sacred vow made at the Temple altars, and she had always kept this covenant. Would this be the breaking point?

I pressed on...

"I don't believe it," she repeated. She began to fluff up the pillows on the sofa in the living room, then changed the subject abruptly. "What's your lesson on this Sunday, Tony?" She didn't want to face this moment.

"I need to move out of this Ward," I said in response. "It would be too overwhelming for Mom if they called her into a court on me. And what about you and the kids?" I'd asked more than any man has a right to ask of the woman who loves him above all others. I reached to touch her, but she instinctively moved away, then realized what she'd done and tried to hide it by walking to the window to look out. I had suddenly become foreign to her, a stranger. She'd thought she knew me.

"Do you want me to come with you?" she asked.

"I still love you, Laura. I'll always love you. I can't leave you here with three children and a new baby. Nothing's changed. Of course I want you to come with me."

"Nothing's changed? Tony, how can you say that? You stand there and tell me you're..." She hesitated as if it were almost as hard to pronounce the word as it was to accept its reality. "You tell me you're gay and then you say nothing's changed?"

She was right. Her whole world had been inverted, twisted, stripped of meaning. I was her world. And by telling her I was gay, I not only deprived her of me, I wrenched her entire religious foundation from her as well. In our understanding of God's plan, a man and a woman can only reach God together. She couldn't do it without me. In the Mormon concept, women have their eternal identity grounded in the righteousness of their husbands—heaven is unattainable without the patriarch of their home. To Laura, I was robbing her of her Eternal reward.

Laura and I had been a part of each other for so long. But, now she also could see that she had to stand alone. Just as I'd seen I'd have to stand away from the Church. I could see the decisions being made in her mind as she spoke. From now on she'd also have only God to look for direction. She turned to face me, her face serious. She said, "You're right, as usual. We'll just have to move out closer to Los Angeles—some place where nobody knows us. You can make a clean break from the Church and be done with it.

Even as we moved our home to the coast, I wondered if the Church wasn't right, after all. I wondered if it wouldn't be better for all of us, especially Laura, to find another man. She needed another man so she could be sealed in the temple to a normal, heterosexual man who could take her with him to the highest glory of the celestial kingdom of God. She deserved much more than I could offer. My mind accepted the prognostications of doom. My mind told me that all that Dale Hansen, Bill Detton, and those months in the archives had taught me were mere rationalizations. I found myself accepting the idea that rationalization was my effort to cover up my sins. I thought of my children almost every waking minute of those weeks and months when I expected to be excommunicated from the Church. I often thought to myself that getting out of their lives at this early age would be the best thing that I could do for their spiritual welfare. After all, I had bought into the view of my utter ugliness in God's eyes and I didn't want them to have someone like me around them to influence them for evil.

It was Rafael's eighth birthday and he would be the last of my children that I would be allowed to baptize in the Mormon Church. It was a thrill for me to dress in white with my son. I loved him and I was so proud of him that day. Like our oldest son Joseph, Rafael had prepared well. As we dressed, I thought, "What will he learn to believe about this man that baptized him today?" I loved him so much. I just didn't feel worthy of being with my beautiful children and my faithful Laura.

Laura and the children attended church alone after that. I continued to meet other gay people. Laura was a real "trooper" and we would argue about theology. But, pretty soon she couldn't try that anymore, neither did I. We were too far away from each other. We were fast becoming like mere roommates with different perspectives on life, instead of husband and wife. She sought counsel from our current Bishop, but didn't share with me what he'd said.

One night after we'd finished dinner, the doorbell rang. Joseph and Lynne were working on their homework at the old kitchen table while Rafael finished the dishes. Laura was rocking Raquel to sleep. She went to the door, the baby in her arms.

"It's the entire Bishopric, Tony," she said. "They want to talk to you, but they won't come in."

I didn't need them to come in. I knew well enough what they wanted. I'd been where they were too many times myself.

"Brother Feliz," the Bishop said, handing me a sealed envelope, "this is a summons to a hearing before a Bishop's court of the Beachside Ward of the Church to inquire as to why you and Laura are divorcing."

"I'm sorry, Bishop," I responded, "but you have no jurisdiction over me. I don't recognize your authority." I held the higher Priesthood, and if I was to be tried, it would be before the proper high council court.

I closed the door. "I'm not going," I told Laura. "And I don't want you to go either."

"Why not?"

"Do you know what will happen there? Do you know what they're going to do?"

She shook her head.

"They'll ask you to testify against me, Laura. I won't have those men getting into any affair that's none of their business. Don't you think that my confusions have put you through enough?" I had asked too much of her already. I had hurt her too deeply. I didn't want her to suffer any more than necessary. Having to testify to a court of the Church, would only cause her suffering. There was no way I could make up for the pain I'd already caused her. I wished I could tell her I knew that. "What we have is none of their concern. It's just between you and me."

The baby was asleep in Laura's arms. She carried her into the bedroom and laid her softly in the waiting crib. I followed. I saw a tear drop land on Raquel's dark curls as Laura pretended to straighten the blanket over the sleeping child. This one would never even know her father. I knew it and Laura knew it.

"Do you agree?" I whispered. "You won't go, will you?"

She walked back into the hallway without answering and carefully closed the bedroom door before she looked at me. Her voice was quiet and controlled when she spoke, as if she spoke to a stranger. "No, Tony. I won't go and testify against you."

The court was held. The verdict: Antonio A. Feliz was "disfellowshiped for disobedience and conduct unbecoming a member of the Church." I moved out of the house and Laura's new attorney contacted me about finalizing the divorce. I was in such an emotionally disturbed mental state that I couldn't answer her attorney's question about who my attorney would be. The badgering I had received in the process of being disfellowshiped had taken its toll. I had begun to function irrationally.

The badgering continued: Excommunication followed soon after. This time I was not even notified beforehand. The letter containing the decision of the court was mailed to Laura's address, even though it was Church policy to send such a letter to the address of the excommunicated party. The Bishop had my new address, but he'd mailed the official letter to Laura. She let me in to open it.

"What is it, Tony?" she asked.

The words blurred as I tried to read. It didn't matter anyway, I tried to tell myself. The Church was wrong, I said to myself. What it was teaching was only hurting people, destroying people. If I sincerely believed it was true and that this action would have an effect on my eternal salvation I'd repent, wouldn't I? However, I wasn't going to change; I knew that. Were they right? Was I one of those unclean things that had no place in the Kingdom of God? Had God separated Himself from me? Did He now want nothing to do with me? If I believed the Church was true, I was spiritually dead. If I didn't, then it didn't matter what they did. But it just wasn't as easy as yes or no; the truth was caught somewhere in between.

I brushed my stubborn tears away. The courts I'd held as Bishop weighed heavily on my mind. We'd always taught they were "courts of love." It wasn't true. Yes, there had often been a rich outpouring of love there. I'd loved those people who had come before me. My counselors had loved them. But in the institution that promoted these courts there was no love at all. How could there be love in any institution that demands absolute loyalty, and enforces this loyalty through manipulation and fear? The fact that many of those courts were filled with love was in spite of the court system, not because of it. The love is original to the people doing their ecclesiastical jobs; the institution doesn't know it. I remembered the many high councils on which I had served and the high council courts we had convened therein. Some of us had loved the accused, but not all of us. I could remember all too vividly how some of my fellow High Councilors had a real sense of bigoted disgust for the accused in those courts. I anguished inside. "They're the ones who are guilty of 'unchristian-like conduct,'" I said bitterly, handing Laura the letter. As long as the institution insisted on fostering its discipline through its Church court system, it would continue to feed prejudice, hatred, bigotry, and yes, exactly that for which it was so quick to condemn its members: "unchristian-like conduct."

"But what else could they do?" Laura asked. "They were just doing what they had to do." She handed the letter

128

back to me without reading it. She knew well enough already exactly what it contained.

As I held up the letter, my hand was shaking nervously. I sensed my heated anger getting out of control.

"Oh, Tony, you're shaking. Are you alright? Do you need to see a doctor?

It's the Church, don't you see? They're making me like this. You asked what they could do besides just hold these damned courts, well, I'll tell you what they could do," I hissed out through my anger, "I'll tell you what we need in the Church. What we need is such an overwhelming outpouring of love for people in distress—people like me," my whole body was shaking now, "such an outpouring of love for people who find themselves outside the rules of the institution that they'll still feel comfortable in being with the members of the institutional Church in spite of their differences. That's what true 'Christian-like conduct' would be."

"Can't you see, Tony, you need to repent."

"All I know is that they are not Christian in this type of action. I don't want any part of them anymore. I just want to have it all over and done with." As I turned to get out of the house and into the car, I added, "Tell your attorney that she should go ahead with everything. I can't think well enough to work with an attorney of my own."

Millions of human beings, our brothers and sisters, are waiting for our help. We cannot help them until we have ourselves overcome...Henceforth, all our striving, if we strive at all, will be that, as the days pass by, we may grow juster and fairer and purer, more kind and more true, move silent and more humble and, having attained ourselves, to point the way to the younger souls coming after us. It is the only means we have to repay the blessed Masters for their Sacrifices.

Elias Gewurz
Ancient Treasures of the Ancient Qabalah

Chapter 8
Justice Lost,
Affirmation Found

Coming out can be a slow process. The plant pushes its way from the seed. The bud unfolds into the blossom. Accepting what one is and becoming what one is destined to be are never accomplished without struggle. Sometimes our heads know things our hearts simply cannot feel and sometimes our hearts understand things we are unable to articulate, but that we nonetheless know with an absolute certainty to be true.

So it was with me. During those first intimate days with Dale in Sacramento, Dale had told me over and over again that it was not a sin to be gay. Many others who cared deeply had also tried to teach me that expressing love is good regardless of the gender of the the two people who share that love. They all tried to tell me that being gay and expressing it was not right or wrong or good or evil. It simply was. Some people were gay; some people weren't. It had nothing to do with righteousness or sin. My head knew it, I think. Logically and reasonably, I knew that I wasn't a bad person just because I was gay and found it natural to express my affections to another man. I had faults, certainly. I made mistakes like anyone else. But I just could not feel that I was intrinsically evil. At least, I didn't feel that way all of the time.

I could tell myself that again and again. I could remind myself of the good I had done in my life. I could remember the people whose lives I'd blessed. Yet still, down deep inside me somewhere was a part of me that felt unclean and somehow

131

unworthy—a frustrated butterfly that refused to fly, convinced that caterpillars were somehow not made to become released from their eternal crawling.

When Laura and the children and I moved to the coast, before my excommunication and our divorce, we'd agreed that Laura and I would try to find out what this gay issue was all about. We began to read up on the subject. I learned much, but in my caterpillar mind, I still refused to call the help-line that had been set up by Affirmation, the social and support group for gay and lesbian Mormons in Los Angeles. After all, I reasoned to myself, it must be an "apostate" organization if they openly defy the Church. Somehow, contacting an openly gay Mormon group was inappropriate for me, a former Bishop. The fact that I had slept with another man just didn't seem to be the important factor; the important thing was that Affirmation must be intrinsically evil. When I finally did call, it was only because of the actions of my Bishopric in my disfellowshipment. It was after I had been disfellowshiped but, before I'd actually seen the letter which had been sent to Laura's home that we began to visit Affirmation meetings in Los Angeles. I was in pain. I hadn't yet realized exactly how much I was suffering, though.

I met Carl Solani through Affirmation. He invited me to share an apartment with him and a friend and, because of the state of my finances at the time, I jumped at the chance. Perhaps one of the most significant things that happened while I was with Carl was that he encouraged me to begin keeping a journal again, something I hadn't done since my days as an active Mormon Bishop.

As I wrote, I found my mind going back again and again to the same themes I'd been drawn to when I worked at the Church Offices in Salt Lake City: the Law of Consecration and Stewardship, the nature of true religion, the core principles of the gospel—truths that would remain when all the cultural trim and excess had been stripped away.

Justice Lost, Affirmation Found

One night, unable to sleep, I took my journal out on the small balcony overlooking Hollywood and began to write:

I've been reading the New Testament again. I'm trying to understand just exactly what I, as an excommunicated holder of Priesthood, can do even though I can't receive the Lord's Supper in church, or exercise my Priesthood office in the church. James, the apostle, has given me the answer: "Pure religion and undefiled before God and the Father is this, to visit the fatherless and widows in their affliction, and to keep himself unspotted from the world." Of course, everyone can visit the fatherless and widows "in their affliction," or in other words, care for the poor and the needy, as well as keep themselves unspotted from the world through the basic commandments to love God and fellowman. Perhaps, James felt that the fullness of the gospel expressed in these simple terms "undefiled" by theologies upon theologies was religion in its "pure" form. We, as gay and lesbian men and women who have been excommunicated, should strive to show our love for God by caring for the poor and the needy (boy, are we the "needy") and living as we each feel is right within our own hearts. We need to love one another and be positive with one another and, most of all, we need to avoid those things which Christ abhorred: hypocrisy and double-mindedness.

I looked up at a sound inside the apartment. Apparently, Carl hadn't been able to sleep either. He came out to the balcony and stood looking out at the lights below us.

"Writing in the journal again, huh?" he asked.

"Yeah. Thanks again for telling me to do this. It helps."

He glanced at the scrawled pages. "So, are you going to tell me what kind of profound truths you're writing down in there?"

It was still hard to put it all into words. My thoughts were such a tangled knot. The journal was my effort to resolve my jumbled thoughts. I handed him the journal and let him read what I'd just written.

"Pure religion," he repeated. "Tell me what you know about pure religion."

133

"When I was working for the Church, Carl, we tried to focus on what 'pure religion' was. We had to, so we'd know what the minimum was that members of the Church in some eastern bloc totalitarian state absolutely had to do in order to live the gospel. But now, it's as if I'm trying to do that for myself, not for some stranger I don't even know." I wondered if he could see the difference.

He did. "It's not so hypothetical now, is it, Tony? It's real. You're the one who needs to know for yourself what the essentials are." He handed the journal back to me and turned again to look over the balcony. "You know, it's funny in a way. We're the ones who're supposed to be living in a free country, a place where freedom of religion is a basic human right. But, sometimes it just doesn't seem that way at all."

I wasn't sure exactly what he meant.

"How free are you to exercise your freedom of speech and your freedom of religion?" he asked. "Are you free to worship God according to the dictates of your own conscience as a whole and complete gay person?"

I didn't answer.

"Well, are you, Tony?"

I wasn't, not really.

"What's keeping you from it? What's stopping you from worshiping the way you want to as an honest, loving gay person?"

But how did I want to worship? Did I even know? Yes, I did know. I wanted to go to the Temple. I wanted to be filled with the peace of that place again and to have my mind opened as it had been so many times before. I wanted to see anew my connection to Eternity in the movements of my hands and the words of my lips, and in that moment of seeing, I wanted to know surely and exactly what this mortal existence needed of me as well. That's what I wanted.

I wanted to bless others. I wanted to put my hands on the heads of those I loved, as I had before, and feel the power of God in me as the words came sure and strong and often surprising. I wanted to use the Priesthood I'd been ordained to

134

use. I wanted the right to call on the powers of heaven in holy places. I had been called. I wanted to be chosen. I wanted...but some of the things I wanted I couldn't say even to Carl.

He repeated his question, speaking slowly, as if he were prompting a child who's forgotten his piece in the school play "What's keeping you from doing that?"

It wasn't the Church that was stopping me. Not really, although I'd tried to blame it. All it could do was mistakenly teach that I shouldn't use my Priesthood, falsely assert that I wasn't worthy to use it. But did I have to believe them? I had covenanted with God, not a church. My Church was the vehicle of a covenant I'd made with God; but, by excommunicating me, the Church had become an inoperative vehicle to me.

"Look at it this way," Carl explained. "It's sort of like polygamy. It's like when Wilford Woodruff issued the Manifesto."

I frowned, not seeing the connection. "Okay, I give up. How is it like that?"

"In 1890, President Wilford Woodruff, as President of the Church, told the world through the Manifesto that the Church no longer practiced polygamy."

"Yes, Carl," I said, just a little sarcastically. "I think most of us are vaguely aware of that."

"And then after that, the Presidents of the Church had to issue additional manifestos to quell the rumors that plural sealings were still being solemnized by their authority."

"Other manifestos?"

"Yes, there were several. And can you imagine why?"

"Well, of course. They had to prove the Church wasn't breaking the law."

"But, they were, Tony! Publicly, the President of the Church had prohibited any more plural marriages. Privately, among holders of the sealing power of the Priesthood, it was still being done. In Mexico or Canada and other places where they were beyond the reach of the law. That's how those old Mormon Colonies in Canada and Mexico got started in the first place. Was it a true principle or not, Tony?"

"I don't know." I couldn't see what he was getting at.

He explained that the Apostles and others of that time had taught that they had been given Keys or authorization by the President of the Church, Keys authorizing them to perform plural marriages, even though these sealings were expressly prohibited by the law of the United States and "officially" by the Church leaders. These same men, however, were not only leaders of the institutional Church. These men were also all a body of Priesthood quorums, and acted as such in an independent fashion outside of the institutional Church. Joseph Smith had done exactly the same thing. He had instructed the Church in public, while in private he shared the mysteries of the Kingdom with those of the "inner quorums" who were ready to receive them.

"So," he continued, "the Apostles and others after the Manifesto taught openly those concepts that were acceptable to the territorial sheriffs and other officials, while in private they continued to seal plural wives to their husbands. The Kingdom of God had retreated into the Temples of God!"

"Well, I remember that when I was spying for the Church on a polygamist group in Salt Lake City, they taught me about what the First Presidency was doing in 1894, just after the Manifesto of 1890. They showed me a document which quoted President George Q. Cannon encouraging the Twelve Apostles to continue on in their sealings of plural unions. I remember that it was dated April 5, 1894." But, I still couldn't really see what any of this had to do with us today.

"Two things, Tony. First of all, it shows us the early leaders of Mormonism saw a difference between the institutional Church and the Kingdom of God, the Holy Priesthood."

"And second?"

"This is what I've been trying to get to! Some of those men were excommunicated. It didn't matter! The Church had to excommunicate them for practicing polygamy, but it didn't change anything for them. They still felt a personal sense of duty to continue in their Priesthood duties, regardless of what the Church did or said."

Justice Lost, Affirmation Found

I began to understand his point. And, strangely, I realized I'd remembered reading other references to this very thing in the journals and diaries I'd studied while doing research in the archives. I'd just somehow never quite made the connection. The polygamists that I'd associated with when I was spying on them for Elder Mark E. Peterson's office had once spoken of this exact concept, but I hadn't made the connection then either.

Carl was silent for a moment while I let it sink in. "So," I said finally, "the Church was an institution and because it was, it did what it had to do to survive—which, in this case, was to go along with what the government demanded."

"They were going to lose the Temples otherwise. It's not really even important to me if they did the 'right' thing or not. The important thing is that I have just as much 'right to use my Priesthood now as those excommunicated members did then. Any of us do, as God inspires us with that impulse through His spirit. That power, the Holy Priesthood, comes from God. Men can't take it from us. All they can do is decide they don't want to allow their institution to acknowledge what we do through its power."

For a moment, it was almost as if I were hearing my own words. Hadn't I taught Jeff the same thing when I'd been working with him to have his temple blessings restored? But somehow I had never realized that that same truth applied to me as well.

I'd accepted the fact that following my excommunication, I was deprived of the right to use my Priesthood. It was a difficult shift of mind to realize I might have been wrong in my acceptance of that sentence. "Well, it makes sense," I said at last.

"Hey, there's something I want to show you." We went back into the apartment and Carl searched through the bookshelf in his living room. Finally, he found the little book. He turned to a revelation John Taylor, the Mormon President who had succeeded Brigham Young, had received in 1886 when he was President of the Church. "By this time, Tony,

137

there had already been several versions of a manifesto suggested to President Taylor. Remember, Wilford Woodruff was President in 1890, just a few years after this revelation came." We read it together.

"...and how can I revoke an everlasting covenant for I the Lord am everlasting and my everlasting covenants cannot be abrogated nor done away with, but they stand forever.

Have I not given my word in great plainness on this subject? Yet have not great numbers of my people been negligent in the observance of my laws and the keeping of my commandments, and yet have I borne with them these many years: and this because of their weakness, because of the perilous times, and furthermore, it is pleasing to me that men should use their free agency in regards to these matters."

"Tony," Carl said seriously. "I think that really is what God wants us to do. To learn to determine for ourselves the right way for us to go. To discover our own path to true spirituality in spite of institutionally prohibited relationships."

He was right. God would never want us to stop functioning faithfully on behalf of others and ourselves. Joseph Smith hadn't been homophobic. If he'd been alive today, I probably would not have been excommunicated. I was no different than the faithful polygamists who found they had to choose between following the institutional Church or their personal conscience. How could a church, an institution, a temporary, mortal institution take from me the power I'd been given to act in the name of God? I had only lost the authority to act in the name of the Church!

No mere organization could take from me eternal temple endowments of knowledge and power that had been sealed upon me before God and angels at the altars of God. The Church was powerless to do it. My mission in life was not changed by whether or not I was a member of any particular church. Just like Lyman Wight, one of Joseph Smith's original Twelve Apostles, who had received a mission from Joseph Smith before his death to take a group of the saints down to

Texas and colonize and build a Temple, I also had been given a mission by God through his anointed. Just as Lyman Wight, one of the original Twelve Apostles who served under Joseph Smith, had been excommunicated for doing what he thought was right, so also had I been. Lyman Wight had acted according to the dictates of his own conscience. I needed to do the same thing.

Carl walked into the kitchen and poured himself a glass of milk. "You know, I think you do have a mission, kid," he said solemnly. He raised the glass to me in a kind of a toast. "Don't let anything get in the way of your finding out what it is. And when you find out, 'Do it!'"

He went back to bed. The eastern sky glowed with the first hint of morning. I watched as the stars faded and the wisps of clouds caught the red glory of the day's coming light.

The gospel was meant to be something very intimate and personal between the believer and God and no one else. Carl had helped me remember that I could trust my own feelings. That, in fact, it was essential for me to learn to discern truth for myself rather than to trust the moralities laid down by any institution. Institutions exist to help teach principles and to administer sacramental ordinances in community to those who believe in them, but they simply cannot confer spirituality on anyone. Becoming one with God must be a personal and individual matter.

I'd been excommunicated. But I was finally beginning to see that they had been wrong. As all of us, I was like the man Lot of the Old Testament. My stay in Sodom, or the world, was only temporary. I had learned that I was a sojourner in the world as Lot was in Sodom. My stay in my "Sodom" was only a stopover point in a much longer journey.

The sky was light when I finally put the journal away and fell asleep.

I continued to read, to pray, to write, and to have long discussions with Carl. It seemed whenever I had a quiet moment alone, his question returned to torment me. What really was keeping me from living the gospel the way I knew I had covenanted to do? What was keeping me from doing good to my fellowmen? From bearing witness of the truths of the gospel as taught by Joseph Smith and others?

One day the naked and unconcealable reality struck me with undeniable force: God wasn't keeping me from that ministry, and neither was I. And if neither God nor I was keeping me from it, then who was running my life?

I determined to make some changes.

I found myself reading the scriptures with a new urgency, confident that these words contained a key, that there was something here we'd long overlooked, and that it was something of profound significance. I was drawn to Moroni's teachings just as I had been the last time I spoke to my Ward in Utah. I read his commentaries on charity over and over.

"Wherefore, cleave unto charity, which is the greatest of all, for all things must fail -

But charity is the pure love of Christ, and it endureth forever: and whoso is found possessed of it at the last day, it shall be well with him.

Wherefore, my beloved brethren, pray unto the Father with all the energy of heart, that ye may be filled with this love..."

To be filled with this kind of love was a gift from God. That gift included the ability to love ourselves, to accept ourselves as Christ accepts us. Sincere and honest leaders in a church might ridicule, condemn, and excommunicate because of the society in which they live and the culture through which they have come to understand the gospel, but certainly God is not and never could be limited by that kind of blindness.

I remembered again what Dale had told me: "God loves gay people too." I hadn't been able to believe him then, but gradually the truth of what he'd said became more and more clear to me. The problem for Mormons who are gay and lesbian, I found, is that we'd been raised to want and expect more than love from our God. We've been conditioned to believe that we, somehow, are a "chosen" people who will become exactly like God—vested in complete bodies of flesh and bone, capable of producing progeny eternally through a kind of Divine heterosexuality. We had been told that God loves us all, but only the worthy will become exactly like Him and His Eternal Bride...like Them, able to stay in their heterosexual relationship in heaven. The hidden message was that it would take more than the "mere love of God" to become like Him and meet our reason for being. I began to see what I'd never seen before. I began to understand that we had, in a very specific and systematic way, accepted a concept of God that promoted our own self-hatred if our inner nature didn't add up to that concept.

Because of that concept, we placed an awful guilt on ourselves that ran much deeper than most fundamentalists' guilt. We let this belief in our innate inability to become heterosexual gods block us from developing love and faith unto which we are all called to grow, especially any expecting to be "Heirs of God."

Now, however, in conversations with Carl, I discovered a truth in the pure gospel that I had missed in the Mormon Church that placed at its center a heterosexual Heavenly Father and Mother. With that concept of the Divine stripped away, the truth was now obvious: as long as we continued to hate ourselves, it was impossible for us to reach out to others in love. And learning to reach out in love was what this life is all about. We must learn that before we can become "joint-heirs."

"Carl!" I said excitedly to him one morning. "I have it!" I tried to put it into words for him so he too could see the amazing truth it had taken me so long to come to. "It's a truly uncluttered view of self, a true view, the view Christ has of us, that allows the power within us to be activated. We have the power to love like Christ does, and to teach others to see themselves in a new light, a purer light. It's by loving that way that we become pure in heart."

141

He laughed and grabbed me by the shoulders. "Ah, Tony," he said. "What a man! Even if it does take you an awfully long time to learn some things. Now go," he added dramatically, pointing out the open window to the streets and houses below us. "Now go, and 'cast Satan out of their midst'!" Carl's effort at comical theatrics was a call. It was a challenge. Teach what you know, share, love, don't be afraid anymore.

I looked where he pointed. There were people out there who were hurting, people who were lost and afraid, people who'd accepted the lies and accusations of those around them, people who didn't know which way to turn. People like the me I'd been only a few short months before. I wanted to tell them what I knew.

I wanted to tell them that God did not condemn them for their sexuality. There were other things of far greater import to God than that. I wanted to tell them that Jesus Christ did see each of them individually through the eyes of a charity that does not ever fail. He wanted us to pray to be filled with this same kind of love.

I wanted to tell them that I could see the power, the energy, the talent that so many of them were blessed with. I wanted to show them the tremendous force for good they could unleash on the world if they could but free themselves from their self-inflicted guilt.

They were my people and I loved them.

Feeling a need to help others who were struggling to accept themselves, others who were perhaps experiencing some of the same kinds of problems I'd experienced, or other serious problems of their own, I volunteered at AIDS Project Los Angeles. It was through this program that I met Luke, an inactive Mormon. He was diagnosed with ARC, but refused to accept the diagnosis. So when he and his lover invited me to move in with them, I agreed, feeling this might be the best way I could help him. Somehow, deep within myself, I sensed that

Luke hadn't been totally honest with us. I seemed to feel that he'd actually been diagnosed with AIDS, not just with ARC.

"Luke," I said once, after trying every other approach I could think of to get him to face the truth about what was happening to him, "Try to look at AIDS in a spiritual context. If you can, I think it'll help you."

Silence.

I wanted to help him. I wanted to share with him a little of what it had taken me so long to learn about myself and about my reality. I tried to imagine what I'd feel like if I'd just found out that I was going to die. I knew that even if I couldn't really know how he felt, I had to try to share with him what I did know. My reality had evolved so much; I had to try.

"We're all beings of mind, spirit, and body, Luke." I tried to explain. "You're so much more than this body." This insubstantial body could grow feeble and weak and sick. Its organs could give out. Its immune system could fail. But no matter what happened, that which was essentially Luke would persist. "Look at it in the spiritual context," I begged. "It's the only perspective that's genuinely grounded. Nothing else about us continues on as it is now."

He wasn't listening. I wanted to show him that he could rise above his depression. I wanted to help him see that it was only through a truer and more earnest way of looking at things than he currently had, that he could ever hope to see the meaning in what he was going through.

But he wasn't ready to hear me. About a week later, he and I were alone in the apartment, and I decided to try again. The newspaper headlines that day were about AIDS in Africa. I showed him the article. "Look, Luke, the first cases of AIDS reported in this country were in the gay community, but in the nations of Africa, it's been a predominantly heterosexual disease all along. Look at this." I set the paper beside him.

He walked out of the room.

"Damn it, Luke!" I yelled through his closed door. "If you don't get a more positive attitude about yourself, it could prove to be fatal to you! Why do you hate yourself so much, anyway?"

Stereo music began from within his room.

143

I knew he couldn't continue on as he was. I pleaded within myself for some inspiration as to what to say that would be a key into his suffering. "Luke, you are not being punished by God in this disease. If that were true, why is God punishing all the little Black children with sickle-cell anemia?"

The door opened.

Luke stood there staring at me as if he were looking at the ugliest sight he'd ever seen in his life. The mean scowl on his face could almost have killed.

Fear began to take hold of me. His look reminded me of some of the mentally deranged people I had met in my life. What should I do? What will he do if I go on? "AIDS has long since leaped over the boundaries that exist between gays and other peoples. Heterosexuals get it too. Children get it. Luke, it's not a gay disease. It's not the wrath of God either!"

He kept on standing there with that ugly scowl on his face. I realized that, in his present condition, I might as well talk to a wall. None of my facts seemed to matter to him. He just stared out, out away from himself. He believed that he deserved to die because he was a homosexual. "After all," he'd said to me once, "I've been excommunicated and I'm now suffering the buffetings of Satan."

Luke could not hear me. He was beyond hearing words. He'd convinced himself that he deserved to be sick. He believed that it was only right that a person such as he should "suffer the wrath of God on earth." Try as I might, I could not convince him otherwise. The following several weeks were some of the most depressing of my entire life. It was so clear to me that Luke's personal *agreement into* his institutionally-imposed guilt was his real disease.

Luke died without a renewal.

After Luke's death, I became more and more aware of others around me who were also dying of AIDS. It seemed that every week I would find out from a friend or from the obituaries that someone else whom I knew personally had passed on. Reading the obituaries had always seemed to be something that people in their seventies or eighties did. But I was in my thirties. My friends whose names I read in those columns had been in their twenties and thirties! The stark nakedness of the fact that we are very frail and perishable creatures, irrespective of our age, began to become part of my everyday thinking processes.

I found myself on the telephone frequently after that. I began to reach out and try to locate misplaced friends who were also gay. I was concerned that others with whom I'd been intimate might possibly have the disease. The idea of coming down with AIDS became a conceivable scenario for me and I began to feel genuine fear.

Doctors had talked with me about sexual dysfunction before when I was married. I had never had the problem of impotency in my life. However, I found myself consciously thinking of not having sex with anyone anymore out of a real terror for my life. I began to ask myself another provoking question: "What if I already have?" What if I am a carrier of this disease and I've infected someone else? Horror overtook me. I began to have nightmares. I saw faces of loved ones—dead faces. I woke up nights screaming out in fear. My pillow was soaking wet from my tears the next morning.

I determined to read and study up on what could be done to prevent the passing on of this virus. I purchased condoms, but I got frustrated when I tried to use them. Sex became a trauma for me. What had, in recent years, become such an important part of my self-concept, had again become my pain—my avenue for manifesting self-hatred.

I stopped.

My nights were so lonely.

Is this what I'd left my wife for? I began to ask myself some questions that I had mentally already begun to think were solved. Although I had insisted to Luke that AIDS was not a punishment from God, deep down inside I now had the same fear—that this terrible disease was nature's punishment, God's punishment for my decision to live my homosexual nature. I began to wonder if God was playing with me, like a chess player. Was my life just a game to God?

Out of the Bishop's Closet

Ugliness came. All my old guilt—the painful guilt I'd thought I had let go of, came washing back over me, relentless and unstoppable. Dale Hansen had said to me back when he and I spent those first four wonderful days and nights together, that I seemed to pour guilt over myself like water coming out of a shower nozzle. Years later, in the wake of AIDS, I found that my shower nozzle of guilt had become a tidal wave in the midst of a vast ocean of guilt.

Listen to your poets, prophets and songwriters
For when their truths harmonize
They teach most painlessly.

They bleed within and
with their blood
pay for our truths.

But will you listen?
Must you bleed too when you don't heed
the counsel of your
poets, prophets and songwriters?

Yes!
Listen now!
Else witness thy blood flowing...

C. G. George

Chapter 9
The Light Goes Out

I stood in the middle of thousands of people huddled close together. Some were hugging; some held hands. Most had lit candles in cups which they held in their hands out in front of them. It was night on the Castro in San Francisco, California; it was my first AIDS candlelight vigil. I looked around me. I saw others in the crowd who were clinging onto their partners in a way I'd never seen before. These were the persons with AIDS in our mass of people. Some of them looked healthier than I. I wondered how the AIDS had manifested itself on their bodies, "How can they look so healthy?"

Others, every now and then in this mass of the dying, were standing there with deeply insetted eyes, pale faces riddled with sorrow, and with a thinness that shouted out their suffering. In the eyes of one, I saw that same look I'd seen in the old photographs of the dying in the holocaust in Hitler's Germany during the Second World War.

I began to sense their burden. My tearing eyes turned into flowing fountains in my sharing of their pain, their suffering, and their heartache. I wasn't dying. To my knowledge, I had not been exposed to the virus; but I knew I was starting to feel what it must be like to be told by medical practitioners that death is close. In my heart, I felt their pain.

A timeless sense of destiny, fate even, filled the cool night. Somehow it seemed that I had already experienced this emotion-filled awareness of what it meant to be alive, to be human, to be connected in such an immediate and intense way to the strangers who stood around me in the street. I was so much a part of them, and they were so much a part of me. But I knew I hadn't ever felt this feeling before, at least not in my remembrance.

I'd had a similar sense of destiny before—that awareness of timelessness, the feeling that comes when the precious experiences of life are somehow set apart from the mundane of life's play—but this was different from that. This night felt so much like a time that I had rehearsed for, even like a time I had been instructed for somewhere in a far-off arena of learning.

We were all one. My total awareness of our oneness was so overpowering that it nearly suffocated me. For so long we had thought ourselves separate, acted as though we were separate, and now we knew ourselves for what we were: ONE. "Emotion" is not a strong enough word to communicate what I felt. "Passion" also leaves the wonder of that night uncommunicated. I later discovered that what I was feeling was probably the nativity of my spirit-self. My inner self was finally beginning to come into synchronization with my body. It was the coming out party of my soul.

Tears were constant. I stood in the street in the middle of thousands of my people cupping my lit candle in my hands, and I knew that—yes—they were me and I was them. These were my people! Love surrounded us and protected us and drew us to each other.

The speakers were articulate. Their contribution to the evening's moment gave me new insights into my own identity. I was seeing myself not only as a gay man, but also as a member of our community here on planet earth. I was not just a gay Mormon; I was a Child of Eternity. Seeing myself so, I was delivered out of my spiritual womb; I was ready to enter the society of all my brothers and all my sisters.

Like many who come from a Mormon heritage, I'd felt I was striving for what Mormons had always called Zion. But as this night of nights progressed, I was able to see that the true Zion is, indeed, THE PURE IN HEART. I'd repeated these words aloud before. I'd thought I knew what they meant. But as the hours of the vigil lengthened, and we sang and cried and listened together, those well-known words took on an entirely new meaning. Zion is not and cannot be limited to the members of a single sect, church, or religious community. The Spirit of God was on the Castro. I felt it every bit as much as I'd felt it in any other place before, including in my most sacred experiences within the Mormon Church. The people who performed and spoke to us had been called of God. Through them, I was receiving light, truth, and pure intelligence. These had become prophets of God to me. They were vessels of knowledge pouring out their precious life-saving essence. The Holy Ghost encompassed us all, opening our minds as it drew us together in love.

I began to whisper a song to myself during the moments of our quiet together. When I realized what the song was, I knew it fit perfectly with what I was feeling. I had been whispering "The Spirit Of God Like A Fire Is Burning!" This is the Mormon hymn that is traditionally sung at the dedication of a Mormon Temple.

But, this was also a night of pain.

I had experienced pain because, as a gay human being, I had been forced to struggle to make sense of my reality while living in a society that is repulsed by its gay members. On this night, however, I was exposed to quite another kind of pain. It was the anguish of the dying.

The Federal Government had been and would continue to be very slow in allocating sufficient funds for research on AIDS in this country. In addition, the elected representatives, although sometimes outwardly accepting of their gay constituents, had generally been unresponsive to the increasing crisis. Gay citizens were not being heard and it was time for unity, solidarity, and response. This candlelight vigil in the streets of San Francisco was taking place in conjunction with simultaneous vigils in every major city of the country. Knowing that all over the United States, others were gathered just as we were, filled us with an almost overpowering sense of bonding, unity, and community. We were all united that night in our fellowship and our commitment to this fight against a bureaucracy that was ignoring its citizenry. But even more than this, we were finally becoming conscious of the fact that we are a PEOPLE: a people in the true and classic sense of the term. I continued to feel the burden of my kindred who were standing with me at this gathering. "How terrible to know that you are soon to leave your loved ones behind!" My tears continued.

Hundreds of persons had died from AIDS during the twelve months preceding the vigil. A man on the stand began to read off the names of those who'd died. As the names of the dead were read off to us, one name hit me so strongly that for a moment I could hardly see. The lights around me blurred into a flickering glow.

"...Jason..."

Was it possible? Could it have been my Jason? Jason Adams? Jason Adams was from Canada. He was a beautiful man of about twenty-four when I first met him. He had dark hair, almost black, and a light, clear, smooth complexion. With his deeply reddened cheeks and the whitest teeth I'd ever seen, he exuded good health and vitality. He exercised regularly at the gym and had always seemed so energetic. He was the first person to teach me the importance of touch in social and interpersonal interaction. From him I learned that touch could be healing to the soul.

Jason had grown up in a fundamentalist Christian home, but he practiced a form of Zen Buddhism. During the months he and I spent time together, he shared many choice things with me. I was always terribly moved to have him speak about the things that mattered to us most. And he did just that. He spoke much about life, spirituality, and the truth of nature. On one such occasion, he said to me, "Tony, if God wanted to have a very natural means of population control without the terrors of war, violence, and disease, wouldn't God choose a means that was compatible with love?"

"Yes, I think so."

"Well, then," he continued, "Wouldn't homosexuality be a perfect population control system for God when there is no more war, no more violence, and no more disease?"

He was absolutely right. "You mean, honest homosexual love?"

"Yeah, true love." He asked again, "Wouldn't that fit into your Mormon concept of ZION in—what did you call it—your middle world of glory, the glory that existed in Eden?"

Jason and I didn't get into the Mormon theologies of procreation and the need of higher progression, but I had to agree that he had hit on a wonderful concept. In my searching state of mind when Jason and I were seeing each other regularly, his ideas on "God's methods of population control" were refreshing to me.

Through the blur of my tears, I saw them reading off others' names. Each name they read off was a realization of death. More and more, I felt the pain of the Lovers, Parents, Brothers, Sisters, and Friends of each of the dead. An emptyness overcame my being. A profound loss.

"Oh My God! What if it was Jason?" The thought lingered on...

I never did find out for sure if it was the Jason I had known. I thought I had seen him in West Hollywood one night, but I wasn't sure.

I had received much from this spiritual giant as well as from all the others who had helped me along the way. These people were good, honest, spiritually motivated and intelligent kindred spirits. Because of Jason and others like him, I was able to continue up the steep path to wholeness that we all must climb, and continue climbing, until we finally reach the summit.

Perhaps I make it look as though I had solved most of my problems, as if I'd resolved the inconsistencies that had battered at my mind for so long. Maybe I give the impression that I was now ready to forge ahead in a wonderful gay life, loving and accepting and learning as I sought to find my own spiritual path and learn God's will for me. Unfortunately, life is rarely that simple.

Usually, life is hard. We learn—truth is revealed to us in whatever way it is that God speaks to us—and then we forget. Life circles and ebbs. When we come back again to the lessons we've learned before, we're ready to learn them in a deeper and maybe even a truer way. And we do learn, with the continuous circling and ebbing of life. Very much like climbing a spiral staircase, life always takes us upward by taking us back to the same place we were before, only now at a higher level.

And through it all, there are times of pain and times of joy, times of darkness and times of light. I knew now that I was gay. And though my heart told me it was okay to be gay, there were many times when my head still could not believe it. My spirit and my body had synchronized, but my mind had not.

I thought frequently about AIDS in the days following the candlelight vigil. I had a repeating memory of Luke's horror-filled face, a look that could have killed with its darkness. I realized why Luke wouldn't pay any attention to my words. He could sense my polarity, my contradiction. How could he possibly take solace in what I'd said to him back then? For regardless of my words, I had believed just as he did. In my sub-conscious mind, I too had accepted the damnation of hell that AIDS was actually God's punishment. This thought began to cling to my inner mind with fatal intent.

I believed that I did have a mission, that all I had experienced and learned in my life up to this point had been a preparation for something far greater. Knowing this, however, was no insurance against having difficult times, lonely times, times when the awful possibility that perhaps the Church was right would come back to torture me—taunting me that I had no right to be happy, maybe even no right to be alive. I had, after all, been unfaithful to my wife when I'd become intimate with other men. I'd tried to remind myself that my specific covenant of chastity was that I would "*...have no sexual intercourse with any of the daughters of Eve except [my] legal and lawfully wedded wife,*" and that I'd kept that covenant *to the letter.* But such talmudic rationalizing was unbecoming of one seeking a godly life. I was seeing my sin very clearly now; I'd sinned just as any adulterer. I'd adulterated my faithfulness to Laura when my affections and attractions had found their expression outside our solemn covenanted relationship. I'd broken the covenant—in search for self.

I was excited when Mom invited me to a family get-together in Anaheim for Thanksgiving. I looked forward to seeing my children, as well as all of my aunts, uncles, and cousins. Thanksgiving had always been a warm, loving, spiritual time for me, and somehow, I thought it could be the same this year.

Laura and I did not speak much, but the children seemed happy to see me. They were still relatively untouched by our separation and seemed to accept Laura's explanations of why we needed to be apart.

My mother's side of the family is mostly Roman Catholic. At these family reunions, those who'd joined the Mormon Church would huddle in their own conversation groups from time to time and discuss religion. Sometimes, if the host family had a TV room, they'd watch a video of Mormon General Conference or some other Church-related meeting. This reunion was no different.

I went into the kitchen to get myself a glass of water. The aunts on my father's side of the family were there talking with the usual loudness that was typical of our reunions. I had the faucet turned on full force and I couldn't quite hear what was on television in the next room. But, when I turned the faucet off and my aunts left the kitchen, the voice on the television sent me to a place hundreds of miles away...

"I want to leave you my witness, my special witness, of our Savior Jesus Christ..."

I heard a crash of broken glass. The glass I'd been holding up to my mouth had fallen into the sink below. The sink was filled with shattered glass.

"I tell you His is the only Name given under heaven whereby we can be saved..." the voice continued. It was a familiar one. I knew that voice.

My aunt came into the kitchen and started to chastise me for breaking one of her glasses.

"I'm sorry," I said as I listened to the voice from the TV room. I walked out of the kitchen and turned in the hallway toward the group gathered around the television screen.

"It's Elder_____" my uncle said, "come on in and have a seat." My uncle was now serving as Bishop of his Ward in a Mexican town in Baja California, just south of San Diego.

I excused myself. Why had I responded so violently to the sound of Elder_____'s voice? Did I still have such powerful feelings about him? It was then that I realized how much that Apostle had affected me years earlier in his office. And, I knew that I was still not forgiving of him.

At these family reunions, some women of the family usually ended up gossiping about others in some corner of the house. Passing by the huddle of my aunts as I walked down a hallway, I overheard one of them say, "Aren't you afraid that he's molested the boys?"

Was I the subject of their conversation? I was suddenly filled with the hotness of intense anger. "What do you think I am anyway?" I yelled at them, "Why don't you do a little bit more reading up on the subject? Perhaps if you'd get some education, you'd realize that being gay is not an automatic infection with a sadistic desire to molest little boys! Yes, I'm gay. But, I'm not a pedophile!"

"Tony," she said quitely, "We weren't talking about you..."

The Light Goes Out

What a terrible mistake I'd made. Embarrassed, I said I was sorry, but still added, "I'd be more concerned about your husbands than about our little boys."

The accusations had come up often enough through others. It was a subject that recently found me responding in a very defensive and angry manner. I was not a molestor of little boys, I was just gay. But my family was just like any other family in our society; they didn't know that being gay was not a sickness. How could I expect them to think that, as a gay man, I wasn't somehow sinisterly interested in little boys? After a couple of hours, I had finally calmed down.

After our evening meal, one of my cousins pulled me to a private corner of the backyard. "I know about you and the way you're living now, Tony," she said when we were alone, "and I have only one thing to say to you: You stay away from my husband!"

I tried to lighten it with a joke, but she was totally serious.

"Hey, I mean what I'm saying," she repeated. "Stay away from him!"

I'd had more than I could take. What did she think I was? What did she think any gay person was, anyway? People were always thinking that just because you're gay you're out to get every man in the sack before they can say no. And I was tired of the accusations.

"You don't need to worry," I told her with a quick shrug that I had somehow learned to overdo during the days I'd lived with Bill. "He's really not my type, anyway."

She glared at me, horrified. I could almost hear her unspoken question: What is your type?

"But if you want," I offered, "I bet I could teach him a few things for you." At that, I taunted her with more effeminate gestures.

"Let me tell you something right now, Tony," she said firmly. "I don't ever want to see you again. If you come to my house, I'll throw you out personally if I have to!"

Perhaps it would not have been so difficult if I had not always been the one my extended family had turned to for guidance over the years—even in my adolescent days. When any of them wanted a Priesthood blessing or to have a child baptized or confirmed, they'd always turned to me. I'd been their family "patriarch" in the times when their own fathers weren't active in the Church. Whenever gospel themes came up in conversations at the homes of relatives, I was the one who was always asked for the definitive answer.

But now, it seemed they wanted nothing to do with me. Whether it was true or not, it seemed to me that most of my relatives were very uncomfortable at even having me in their homes. So I exiled myself. After all, wasn't I the "bad guy," the "undesirable one" of the bunch? Wasn't I the one who should put himself away so the others wouldn't have to deal with "evil"? Buying into the lie that I was innately evil, I decided to become lost to my family. I stopped going to family reunions. I even asked Mom not to share my address with any of our relatives.

My old feelings of worthlessness began to engulf me once again. Hadn't I destroyed Laura's life? By trying to live a lie as a heterosexual Mormon man in his homosexual closet, hadn't I sown the seeds of her future hatred toward me? I had been no different from the double-minded hypocrites Jesus had cursed in His ministry. Would my children grow up hating their own father?

What was all the theologizing for, anyway? What Carl had tried to teach me about Joseph Smith, what I had taught Jeff in those long-ago days when I was Bishop—that the Priesthood was separate from the Church—none of it seemed to matter any more. What difference did it make in light of my own sins? It was all just talk—an endless stream of empty, meaningless words—and I was sick of it.

Alone at night, I would remember how Dale had held me and comforted me and made my awful guilt go away, at least for a few minutes, at least while I was in his arms. Hadn't I progressed at all since then? That thought depressed me even further. I was what I was and I knew it, but I still could not accept it as a good. If I said I did, I was lying to myself, and I hated myself almost as much for that as I hated myself for being gay.

I was a hypocrite. My body would be what it was-- gay. My mind continued to accuse and pour on the guilt. I was divided. I was a hypocrite. Who was I to try to teach others that it was okay to be gay, that Joseph Smith had, more than anything else, emphasized the liberality of God and the all-inclusiveness of the New and Everlasting Covenant? Who was I to teach, as Dale had, of a God who loved gay people too? Who was I to teach that when I didn't believe it myself....when I couldn't believe it, no matter how hard I tried, no matter how many times I told myself in words that it was true? Who was I, a common hypocrite, to try to teach spiritual truths to others?

I wasn't going to change. Nothing was going to change. Things were only going to get worse. I was a failure, that was all. A total and absolute failure as a husband, a father, a Latter-day Saint, a man.

I had tried and tried to reconcile what I was with what I knew and what I felt, but I couldn't. No matter how I tried, no matter how many times I went around and around with it in my head, it never came together. The only way to make one part of what I knew fit, was to deny another part. And I just couldn't do that anymore. The attempts to do that, both to understand as well as to act as if I did understand, had left me exhausted. I had no will left to struggle with it anymore. And if it was impossible to make sense of my life, then I could see no point in living.

The Church to which I had totally devoted myself and to which I had willingly consecrated all I had, had pronounced me the worst of sinners. To prove this, in its effort to keep itself clean and pure before God, it had "cut me off" from its communion. I was going more and more into agreement with their act of my excommunication.

I was literally in hell. Darkness and pain and fear held me powerless in their awful grip. Ignorance and despair

159

imprisoned me. I wished I could die. No possible existence that would follow this one, no matter how awful it might be, could be any worse than this.

I was gay, and being gay was an awful thing to be, and I was never going to stop being gay. No matter what I did, no matter how hard I tried, I was always going to be gay. How could I go on living? It seemed that anything on the other side of death would be better than this awful pain.

I took out a life insurance policy to cover me in the event of accidental death and named my children as the beneficiaries. When I died, each one would receive enough to finance their missions for the Church and put them through college.

One cloudy Wednesday afternoon, I filled the car's tank with gas and purposely left off the gas tank cap. I started to get onto Interstate 5 heading for the Mexican border, then realized I was not ready yet. There remained one more thing to do.

I called Laura from another gas station. I had made my decision and was ready to die, but before I did, I wanted to talk to her one last time. Maybe there'd been just a moment in all of this experience that had been good—one, just one time when, even gay, even awful, I'd done something worth remembering. Maybe my life had reflected some meaning after all. I was so terribly sorry about all the hurt, pain, and suffering I'd brought to her. It was so clear to me that day that the agony which I'd opened her life to would not end for a long time. Would she see how sorry I was?

She was bitter and angry and hurt. She could hardly talk to me. It would be better for her if I were gone and she could find someone else. Everyone would be better off if I were gone. I got back on the freeway and headed for Mexico.

I was too many people. All my fragmented and disjointed selves fought each other, battling for dominance, while the "I" that was somehow more than any of my separate parts struggled for wholeness. My spirit ached for unity with God, to be lifted, to transcend this temporary plane, to know the mysteries of eternity, to become Infinitely bonded and sealed. My mind was a self-hating, self-defacing, self-destructive entity. It attacked me, condemned me, tried me, and found me guilty a thousand times a day. My body had become a piece of flesh, at once devouring and also being devoured, the scraps thrown away again after each futile attempt to satisfy its lustful appetite. It was only in sex—the singular most intimate function of the physical body—that I felt validated at all, and for that, my mind only condemned me all the more.

A sign marked the exit for Euclid Avenue. It was Anaheim—the town where I was born. It was fitting to pass the place where I'd begun my life on my way to the place where I would end it.

I'd seen the place a few weeks before. The road twisted and curved and beyond the insubstantial guardrail the jagged rocks tumbled their way to the sea. If the crash didn't kill me, or the resultant explosion, then I'd drown, unconscious and bleeding, as the evening tide rose to cover the rocks.

A car honked.

I glanced toward the sound and recognized Chad's familiar white sports car. His presence unnerved me. What was he doing here, driving along beside me? He grinned at me, a smile full of life, radiant and vital and whole, then waved, and took the Euclid exit off the freeway.

I wanted to shout after him. I wanted to make him come back to me. "Chad! Chad!" I was whispering his name aloud. "Don't leave me. Don't leave me alone." His car was out of sight.

He was gone. I was alone. I'd never felt so alone. Was this what death was? This kind of being alone? I didn't want to be alone. The fear of it gripped me, seized me, held me, and would not let me go. A moment before, I had contemplated driving my car over a cliff into the ocean and had known no fear; now, suddenly, I knew what terror was.

My hands clenched the steering wheel. My breath came in rough and ragged gasps. Somehow I maneuvered the car off the freeway. I was crying aloud, sobbing hopelessly out of control. The pain of my separateness clenched me in its grasp. I couldn't get out of it. I couldn't get away from it.

A telephone. I had to get to a telephone. There was a pay phone at the end of the off ramp. Numbly, I pressed Chad's number. The rings were endless. Two rings. Three rings. His voice, then: "I'm not able to come to the phone right now. If you'll leave your name and number..." My fingers were cold as I hung up the phone.

I drove blindly north. All I knew was that I couldn't be alone. I had to find someone. I recognized my cousin's neighborhood. The cousin who had told me she never wanted to see me again. I stopped the car in front of her house, then stumbled up the walk and pushed the bell. She wasn't there, but her husband, after hesitating only a minute, opened the door and invited me in.

"You want a beer?" he offered.

"No. No, I just need to make a phone call."

This time Chad answered. "What are you doing, Tony? Where are you?"

"I'm at my cousin's house in Fullerton. After I saw..."

He interrupted me. "When you get off the telephone, get into your car right away and get your ass over to my place. Will you do it?"

I told him I would.

"On your way here, go to the corner of Euclid Avenue and Ball Road. Go into the market there, buy two filets, then come straight down Ball Road to my place. Don't do anything else. Do you understand? Do you have any questions?"

This was totally unlike Chad, but I didn't question him. I was out of control and I knew it. I put my life in his hands, and did exactly as he'd instructed.

I stayed with Chad for five days. I never left his apartment except to go to the pool or the jacuzzi. Gradually the terror receded. He had been a counselor and therapist, and had been trained to listen. He knew that more than anything else, I needed to talk and receive reassurance of my tie to reality in life.

The Light Goes Out

Chad freely gave me both. Those five days were healing moments for me because of the way that Chad orchestrated them. He had me feeling physical pleasures constantly in the dining room, in the hot tub and in the bedroom. "Why were you so commanding with me on the phone the day I called you? Between you and me, I've always been the active one. Why, Chad?" I asked him one morning as we sat in his kitchen over coffee.

"Oh, I don't know," he answered easily. "It just seemed as if you needed someone to tell you what to do. I guess, at the moment, I wanted you to be passive with me. Why?"

But I didn't really know either. "Why have you let me stay here with you since that night? Usually, I go to my own place. Why did you change our usual way with each other?"

He laughed, as if the reason should be clear enough to me. "I just wanted to, Tony. Is there something wrong with that?"

"You saved my life, Chad."

He set his cup down a little too suddenly. "What?"

"I was on my way to Mexico to kill myself when you passed me on the freeway and waved to me." He knew I was totally serious; this was not the sort of thing one said in jest. "I was ready to do it, Chad. I would have done it if you hadn't... if you hadn't been there." It's true, if he hadn't driven by right at the time he did, I wouldn't be here now. I wouldn't be alive. I wouldn't see this sunshine, dancing warm and quick through the kitchen window. I wouldn't feel my own breath as it filled my lungs, moment by moment making me feel more and more alive. My arms and hands were stretched out on the table in front of us both. I had never known my own fingers were so beautiful, so amazingly alive.

He said that he knew days earlier by the way I was acting that something was going on in my mind that was not healthy. Chad reached to touch my hand with his, then stood and grabbed me to him, embracing me with his whole being. We held tightly onto each other, grateful and wondering, and

163

a little in awe of the forces that had brought us together. The same forces now held us locked in each other's arms, unable and unwilling to break the connection that completed us and reminded us of what it was for two people to be made one. This, then was what life was—to know the meaning of love, to be close and real, to breathe, to search, to learn to save each other and lift each other.

I had been prepared to commit the ultimate sin. I'd been on my way to eternal perdition when Chad was put in the right place at the right time by the tender Divine watchcare I can now see was keeping a faithful vigil. Chad became my connection to this mortal life. Surrounded by the strength of his love, my dischordant and disharmonic selves began to merge and unify. I was slowly becoming whole, synchronized. "Do you see, Tony?" Chad asked. "Do you see what you would have missed if you'd actually gone through with it?"

No unhallowed hand can stop the work from progressing. Persecutions may rage, mobs may combine, armies may assemble, calumny may defame, but the truth of God will go forth boldly, nobly, and independent, till it has penetrated every continent, visited every clime, swept every country and sounded in every ear, till the purposes of God shall be accomplished and the great Jehovah shall say, The Work is done.

The Prophet Joseph Smith
History of the Church, p.540

Chapter 10
Coming Out Spiritually

As I walked up the steps outside the front doors of the Old Stone Church on the Temple Lot in Independence, Missouri, I felt a strangely familiar feeling. A sense of expectation. And yet, at the same time, an odd feeling that I was remembering something that had already happened. I glanced around the grounds to see what might be making me feel this way. Then, as if I'd suddenly remembered something, the words formed within me: "Tony, you're going to hear a Prophet of God speak today." I pulled the door open and went inside.

Feeling the need to make a new beginning following my experiences in southern California, I'd accepted the offer of Tim Gadson, an old friend from my BYU days, and I'd moved to Missouri. I'd gotten work as Director of Residential Life at Park College, a small, four-year liberal arts college. Its main campus was located in a secluded set of beautiful wooded hills just outside of Kansas City, Missouri.

I soon found that many of the people I worked with were members of the Reorganized Church of Jesus Christ of Latter Day Saints, the large branch of Mormonism that did not follow Brigham Young to the west, and I felt a need to find out more about what these people believed. I had taken the opportunity to spend much of my free time in the Library of the Historical Commission of their Church studying Mormon history from their perspective. Again, I was learning that there are always two sides to every story.

As I stepped into the front foyer of the church, the staircase leading to the balcony was on my left. In front of me, the center doors opened into the main floor aisle. I started up the steps and then realized who was speaking. It was a voice I'd heard before on tape, but never in person—President Wallace B. Smith, the President of the Reorganized Church and great-grandson of the Prophet Joseph Smith.

How uncanny, I thought to myself. I had known as I walked up to the front doors that a man called a prophet of God would be speaking. President Smith stood at the pulpit. A glow surrounded him. I was stunned at the sight and for a moment could not move from where I stood. It was the same light I'd seen emanating from President David O. McKay at the Salt Lake City Mormon Tabernacle years before. Only, this time, it was shining from President Wallace B. Smith! The light that radiated from him seemed to spread out until the warmth of it encompassed me as well. A stillness filled the entire room. Mortal sounds were hushed and a voice I'd felt years before resonated through my soul: "Behold, your Prophet."

An usher came up beside me and gently touched my shoulder. "Are you all right, sir?" he whispered. I couldn't speak as I tried awkwardly to brush away my tears of wonder. This had all happened before. I'd seen exactly this same light and had felt the same voice declare the identical words. I stood there with the usher for a few minutes trying to regain my composure. But how could this be?

The next day, I still felt so confused by this experience that I called my supervisor to let him know I wouldn't be able to come to work. I needed to be alone. As I walked toward a part of campus where I'd never been before, the urgent need to make some sense of this experience would not be stilled.

Because of the manifestation I'd received in 1960 when I first met David O. McKay, I had accepted Joseph Smith and the men who'd followed him in the leadership of the

Mormon Church—and only these men—as true prophets of God. Growing up, I had been taught that the Mormon Church was the only true church on the earth and that the Presidents of the Mormon Church were the only true Prophets of God. I'd accepted that teaching. All other people claiming to be prophets of God, it had therefore followed, must be what the scriptures call "false prophets." However, now I had received a witness that another man was also one of God's Prophets. The problem was that this man was the President of another Church, a church that didn't even believe in the ordinances of the holy temple, sacred ordinances that I loved and cherished. This man's Church had rejected these ordinances, these hallowed practices that his own ancestor had initiated, ordinances with which I personally had experienced such marvelous spiritual manifestations.

How could I turn my back on all the things I'd been taught? How could I forget all the experiences that had uplifted and changed me? I couldn't. No, I couldn't deny that all of those experiences had been given to me by God. And yet, President Smith had, just recently, spoken of a new temple to be built by the members of his Church, "a temple of reconciliation, dedicated to world peace." What did it all mean?

I had almost been successful at determining within myself to let the entire belief system that I had obtained through Joseph Smith go. But now this new experience complicated things all the more. Part of me just wished God would leave me alone and let me have my good memories of my experiences in Mormonism and get on with my life elsewhere.

I sought out solitude.

The waterfall in this secluded corner of the campus was especially beautiful. I'd heard of the beauty of this part of the campus, but I'd never before been here. The trees had their spring leaves and the grass and ground cover were emerald in their glory. I could hear the sounds of twigs and last year's leaves being pressed under my feet as I approached the waterfall, but then the thunderous noise of the rushing water

169

drowned out every other sound. The power of the natural undamned water pouring over the rocks at the top of the falls was only outdone by the deafening sound of it hitting the rocks and water below. The sky was its usual clear blue and everything else seemed secure, serene, and in its proper order.

I set the Bible I'd brought with me on a rock as I sat down there in the midst of God's creation. If nothing else did, at least the beauty of this place made sense to me.

I sat and continued to ponder all I could see, hear, smell, and otherwise sense of the wonder of nature which was all around. Why isn't there this kind of order in the movement initiated by Joseph Smith? I thought. The temple. The Prophets. The sealing power of Elijah. The planned temple for which the Reorganized Church was raising money, which even they themselves openly stated would have ministries in it they didn't currently understand.

I couldn't help but recall the words President Harold B. Lee had spoken when he laid his hands on my head in the Los Angeles Temple. As the President of the Church at that time, for a believing Mormon, he was the only one able to pass on Keys —he alone had had the authorization to pass on the sealing power, the power spoken of in the New Testament— the "binding" and "loosing" power of the Holy Priesthood. When he had given me the Keys to use this most sacred of Priesthood powers, he had made a very confusing promise to me that I would never forget: ...*the Lord will enlighten your mind and you will gain a hidden understanding of the deep and far-reaching significance of the sealing power which you have now received...and the day will come when you will use this sacred power on behalf of those of your own kind...*

At the time, Laura and I thought that President Lee must mean that I would be sealing Latin American couples in the temples of God for time and all eternity. But on that day, sitting on a rock by that beautiful waterfall, I had to admit that I'd only sealed two Latin American couples out of all the hundreds who'd knelt before me. Could there perhaps have been another meaning to that promise, a meaning I would only see now after all I'd learned? Could he have been mistaken? Was I?

I remembered the experiences I'd had with President Spencer W. Kimball when I'd worked for the Church Offices in Salt Lake City, Utah. I remembered how I'd come to understand the meaning of "true" in reference to God's holy men to actually mean "ethical." Certainly Harold B. Lee had been an ethical prophet, but God had shown me that Wallace B. Smith was an ethical prophet also. It was such a paradox to me.

My questions continued on and on.

I must have sat on that rock for hours. Finally, as the evening shadows lengthened and a chill touched the damp air, I rose to go back to my apartment. But as I started to get up, reaching for the unopened Bible, I slipped. The book started to skid toward the water; I grabbed for it, almost tearing the pages, but rescued it before it fell. As I began to smooth the pages that had wrinkled, I saw a verse I'd marked with red pencil years before:

Wherefore the rather, brethren, give diligence to make your calling and election sure; for if you do these things, ye shall never fail. 2 Peter 1:10

"...make your calling and election sure...**if you do**...ye shall never fail", the words seemed to ring out in my mind over and over again like the sound of a bell in a church.

"*Charity never faileth,*" Paul had written to the Corinthian Saints. Did "never failing," because of making our calling and election sure, have to do with charity then? I'd always thought it had to do with the temple ordinances and the covenants made there. That's what we'd been taught. I'd always understood that it was through the ceremonies of the temple that a person finally received the "fullness" of the sacramental ordinances which were touted as the necessary factor for one's calling and election. Did the temple covenants have more to do with charity than I'd been taught? Was charity

171

the key principle undergirding temple rites? Wind blew the pages to another verse I'd marked...

For we have not followed cunningly devised fables, when we made known unto you the power and coming of our Lord Jesus Christ, but were eyewitnesses of his majesty.

For he received from God the Father honour and glory, when there came such a voice to him from the excellent glory, This is my beloved Son in whom I am well pleased.

And this voice which came from heaven we heard, when we were with him in the holy mount. 2 Peter 1:16-18

Of course! My thoughts raced at a staggering pace. Jesus was on the holy mount with his *"chosen "* ones. The Father came to Christ and the Apostles. *"By His own voice"*, The Father declared His acceptance of His Beloved Son. I suddenly remembered that Joseph Smith had taught that the final sacrament came direct from God, *"by His own voice."* I suddenly realized that, here, Jesus was going through those exact processes that Joseph Smith taught any of us would have to go through in order to be told *"by His own voice"* by God that our calling and election had been assured. I turned to read a familiar scripture found in the Second General Epistle of Peter, verses 16 to 19 of chapter one: *We also have a more sure word of prophecy; ye do well that ye take heed, as unto a light that shineth in a dark place, until the day dawn, and the day star arise in your hearts.* II Peter 1:19

The ancient Apostle had there recorded that he and his colleagues had *"also"* received their own *"more sure word of prophecy"* themselves. I realized for the first time in my life what was meant by Peter when he'd counseled the saints to *"make your calling and election sure"* (2 Peter 1:10). Joseph Smith had taught that this was only done by God, the Father *"by His own voice"* to those who received it. My mind raced on through all I'd learned.

I now could see with a totally new insight I'd never had before. I now saw what was meant by the phrase about Jesus' need to be baptize*d, "...to fulfill all righteousness"*. On the

Mount of Transfiguration to which Peter here referred, Jesus had received the final act, the consummation of His entire example to all of us. And, He had done it by fulfilling every requirement that Joseph Smith had taught would be required of every one who could expect to be One with Him. I now saw that this final act—this consummation—was also a sacramental ordinance, the Divine Rite. Most importantly, I finally saw the connection of Priesthood sacraments and the need for Christians to also know that the life of Jesus was also a complete example of charity—the pure love of Christ.

Charity was the key principle. His life experience took Him through a mortal journey that required that he receive every sacramental ordinance beginning with water baptism and ending on the Mount in a sacrament of communion with The Infinite. The wonder of my discovery was that love (or charity) was a principle that was woven throughout the fabric of the mortal life of Jesus. Jesus had charity, not only toward others, He had charity toward Himself *also*. The idea lingered on, "Jesus had loved himself even when all others had abandoned him, with the only exceptions of his mortal mother and His Beloved, John."

Suddenly the memory of the day I had marked these verses flooded my mind. I remembered the glorious manifestation, the whispering of beings from the other side. The rushing sound, was that the sound Joseph had written of? Then, without any warning, it was as if I was back in the Los Angeles Temple again, as if I'd gone back in time. I again experienced the profound sense of the all-encompassing love God had for me, the same sweet, complete "unspeakable" love I'd received in the Los Angeles Temple years earlier. Why, why had it taken me so long to believe it?

This place had become a temple to me.

I decided that I would try to hold fast to the basic principles of the gospel as Joseph had taught them. I would trust that I would continue to be directed by God, since I had so obviously been directed by Him thus far. Most of all, I was finally able to decide to just let go. I couldn't make sense of the seemingly contradictory manifestations about the two presidents of the two separate churches. However, I had now been given the faith to bear the burden of uncertainty. I had decided to yield myself to God, and let God manifest God to me without requiring a theological knowledge explaining what was going on.

And so, every day, expecting to receive further knowledge or direction, I went about my work at the college as usual. After all, God had directed me before and He surely would now.

Errands for my job often took me into Kansas City. One such trip had me driving on the freeway going through the downtown area. Not really paying much attention to the road, I suddenly realized I had taken the off-ramp off the freeway. Only somewhat concerned about my daydreaming, I looked for the next street that would lead back onto the freeway. Then, I discovered that I had turned away from the freeway. I drove up to a driveway and pulled into a parking lot to turn around. It was the parking lot of the Roman Catholic Cathedral of Kansas City.

I sat in the car with the motor running.

How bizarre, I thought to myself. I'd asked for further direction from God. Could this be it? I started to walk up the steps to the Cathedral, still with no idea what I was doing there. Once inside, it took my eyes a minute to adjust from the brightness of the out-of-doors. There was a man at the front of the church. He motioned me to come to him. I glanced behind me to see if there was someone else there, but there wasn't.

"Come up here," he invited. "I've been waiting for you." I walked down the aisle toward him, and he greeted me with a warm handshake.

"Waiting for you?" I thought to myself.

Coming Out Spiritually

"Have you decided to be confirmed by me at the confirmation ceremony here in the cathedral next month?" he asked.

"Well, actually, I...I'm a Mormon," I said. I was surprised at the difficulty with which I declared my allegiance of faith.

"Were you confirmed as a Catholic?" he persisted.

"No. I wasn't," I said, still very confused. Did he think I was someone else —maybe someone who had made an appointment to see him, but then hadn't come? "I was baptized as an infant like most Catholics," I told him. "But I wasn't ever confirmed."

Just then, an extremely tall man came out of the sacristy to the left of the main altar. The first man said, "This is Brother Jensen. He was also a Mormon." Then, the first man turned and walked into the sacristy out of sight.

"Do you know who that man is?" Brother Jensen asked.

"No, Who?"

"He's the Bishop of Kansas City and he obviously wants to confirm you."

"But, I've already been confirmed in another church."

"Didn't you just tell him you hadn't been confirmed a Catholic?"

I nodded.

Looking down to me from his towering stance, Brother Jensen said, "The Bishop wants to confirm you. I'd let him, if I were you. You can take catechism lessons from Father O'Hara down at St. Patrick's Church and then you can decide for yourself."

As I walked down the front steps of the cathedral toward my car, I wondered if my mind was playing tricks on me. But, it was as if the Bishop had been waiting for me. I pondered the strangeness of the experience and had a little laugh within myself. It was all so radical.

175

I didn't even notice.

No, as I drove the car, I didn't notice that I was in the downtown streets of Kansas City, not on the freeway going where I had originally been headed. I was driving toward St. Patrick's Catholic Church.

I was baptized in the Reorganized Church at the beginning of April. In my mind and heart, I wasn't just becoming a member. I was acknowledging in public, to God and to myself, that I really had been blessed with a revelation of Divine Will concerning that Church's President. It was my return to Joseph Smith and all that he'd represented to me. It was my declaration that God, indeed, is to be found in Mormonism.

Only a few weeks later, I was confirmed in an elaborate and very impressive ceremony by the Roman Catholic Bishop of Kansas City. This took place in the beautiful cathedral in the company of almost 100 other newly confirmed Roman Catholics. This was my homecoming. It was my rebirth into the church of God which knows no institutional boundaries, the "mystical body of Christ." I was not just a member of both churches, I was finally a part of the inner church that extended beyond institutions.

"I don't understand it, Tony," my friend Ron said one night. "It seems like you want to make sure you're okay with God and that you just want to cover all the bases."

Try as I might, I couldn't really tell him everything. I hadn't told him about the manifestations or about all the details of how I'd been led into the entire situation. But, being a good friend, Ron shrugged his shoulders and said, "Well, all right. I don't understand it, but it's your life."

It was my life. It was my path to travel, to grow closer to that which unites all churches. It was the road not traveled by very many people. It was a way that leads one through a certain understanding that whether they are called "all the angels and saints" or whether they are called "the church of Enoch and of the Firstborn," it is the same. It was the way that let me see Joseph Smith and Saint Ignacius as members of the same Priesthood order. It was, in fact, the way that had its focus on those things that unite the various divergent paths, rather than on those things that separate.

It was a focus on unity in our great diversity. This was the way that did not have to be wide but only very narrow because so few ever used this path. On the other hand,"wide is the way and broad is the gate, that leadeth unto the deaths." It had to be "wide" because the vast majority "go through thereat." The sad understanding that finally came to me was that most of us follow a way that focuses on our differences.

Indeed, I now understood that I'd chosen the *"strait and narrow way"* written about in scripture. I finally understood why "strait" was spelled that way in my King James Bible. It was not "straight" in the sense of a "straight line," meaning the shortest distance between two points. No, now I understood that it meant "strait" in the sense of a "difficult" path to follow, such as a ship navigates through "straits" with caution.

I had changed within, I had finally done what I wanted to do to show my God and myself that I acknowledged His Spirit in all places according to the faith of the people. I was no longer bound by any institutional Church, but only by the Spirit of God. The burden of uncertainty had finally become light to me. In the midst of my confusion, I'd gained the faith to act within them. Again, and most beautifully, I did not require that my mind be able to examine the whole experience theologically.

I'd let go.

Several days after confiding in Ron about my confirmation in the Catholic Church, he asked me something over dinner that seemed almost to be an effort to persuade me that I had made a bad mistake. "Tony, doesn't the *Book of Mormon* call that Church 'the church of the Devil'?"

"How can you even ask that, Ron? You sound like one of my old Sunday school teachers! Why would you revert to a bigoted comment like that? It doesn't sound like you. Ron, it isn't becoming of you."

"Seriously Tony..."

"I am serious." My heated indignant emotions were coming to the surface.

"Hear me out, Tony."

After a big sigh, I made a waving motion with my hand.

"When Paul wrote to Timothy in what is now First Timothy in the Bible, he prophesied about false teachers in the Last Days who would be seduced by *"doctrines of devils...Forbidding to marry,...commanding to abstain from meats..."*

"Oh, I get it. That's supposed to have reference to Roman Catholics because they have a celibate priesthood and because of the old custom of not eating meat on Fridays."

"Well, yes," he said. His manner became a little sheepish. We had known each other for years and Ron could read my face very well; he knew I could not agree with him.

"Thank you for doing what you feel is right as my friend. But, Ron, what I have done is right for me. Let me try to explain something." We read the verses in I Timothy 4:1-4 together and I asked: "Does your church allow you to marry your life's companion?"

"What does that have to do with the scripture?"

"A lot...well, does it allow gays to marry?"

"No, of course not. You know that. None of our churches do."

"Exactly. You see Ron, I believe that Paul was indeed prophecying about our times. Only, I think that his remarks were not limited to any one particular institution. I think he was warning all of us about church leaders forbidding two people in love from having their union blessed by their church, even ours."

Coming Out Spiritually

"You think this is warning us about church leaders not allowing gays and lesbians to get married in any church?"

"Well, does it apply?" The answer was obvious.

"What about 'commanding to abstain from meats'? Only the Catholics do that."

"Correction: did that." It's no longer considered in that way since Vatican II. But, the important thing is that the word "meats" here can also mean "foods" in a generic sort of meaning. If that were a correct interpretation, this passage could include what Brigham Young and some in the Reorganized Church taught about "alcohol, coffee, tea and other counsel in the Word of Wisdom. Remember, it was not originally a *commandment*."

That was the last time that Ron and I argued about my decision to receive the Roman Catholic rite of confirmation. Ron was a good friend, and he wanted to help me avoid any future disappointments. I had been able to calm his fear that my actions would lead me to further heartache.

George and Dean were life companions who lived in Kansas City. Over the previous several months, I had been heavily involved in the birth of a new Kansas City Chapter of Affirmation. Several men in our new group were members of the Reorganized Church. George, however, was not. He was an alumnus of Ricks College in Rexberg, Idaho and was a Mormon of the Utah branch of Mormonism. Frequently, George and Dean would have me over for dinner in a style that was unique to Dean. Dean's meals were always spread on top of every item of furniture they had in their formal dining room. Their Victorian home complete with beautiful oak wood trim was a very pleasant setting for good friends, good food, good music, and wonderful conversation. Dean and I sometimes would compete at baking desserts for those Sunday meals. It was over one of Dean's excellent Dutch apple pies that George finally asked me something he'd been pondering over for almost a full year...

179

"Tony, you were once a sealer in the Mormon Church, weren't you?"

Dean was pouring himself some coffee, "What's a sealer?"

"A temple sealer performs marriages in Mormon temples," George responded. I had listened with sincere empathy for several months now as George would speak to me of his love for Dean and how he'd hoped they could be sealed someday in a temple for all eternity.

I took this opportunity to explain to Dean what the Mormon tradition that George believed in so much taught about marriage: "That only a couple who had received this special sealing blessing on their union could have an eternal duration as a couple. That even death wouldn't terminate their loving relationship."

Dean asked, "How'd you get this power, Tony?"

"From the Prophet," George interrupted. He was so anxious. Dean's eyes met mine in understanding. George loved Dean and Dean loved George very much. Serving himself a second helping of pie, George added, "Only the Prophet can give anyone that sealing power."

While George had the pie in his mouth, Dean asked, "Which Prophet gave you the sealing power, Tony?"

"It was Harold B. Lee." I continued explaining to Dean, who was very much a Roman Catholic, that it was much like the Keys given to St. Peter by Jesus in Catholic tradition. "Mormons believe this is the Priesthood power to 'bind on earth and in heaven' and to 'loose on earth and in heaven.'"

"Does that mean that according to Mormon belief, you have the same authority as St. Peter did?"

"Insofar as sealing unions of couples for eternal duration is concerned," I agreed. After a brief silent moment while George and Dean stared at each other waiting for one of them to say something, it came to me. I suddenly knew mentally what George had been working up to all evening.

Coming Out Spiritually

"Will you seal me and Dean for eternity, Tony?"

I explained that while I believed I did, indeed, still *have* the sealing power of Elijiah, I also believed that I needed to receive additional authorization in order to *use* that power. Until then, I used a bit of Mormon history to advise George and Dean on what they could do. "Willard Richards was one of the closest confidants of Joseph Smith. He was the keeper of Joseph Smith's personal diary and was with the Prophet when he was killed. If anyone had known how Joseph Smith would respond to your question, Willard Richards would've known. He's one of the persons who recorded Joseph Smith's comments about the goodness of two who are very friends sleeping together in each other's arms in the same bed in 1843." I continued explaining that after the death of Joseph Smith, Willard Richards did something that shed some light on what a couple can do when there is no authorized sealer to seal a couple's union for time and all eternity. "In 1845, Willard Richards and a woman named Alice Longstroth used what Willard Richards may have called the 'solemn covenant' method of sealing themselves to one another as though the sealing covenant had been placed upon them." I later found the reference in the research done by Dr. Michael Quinn as quoted in Dialogue, a journal of Mormon history. I sent them the quotation:

At 10. P.M. took Alice L........h [Longstroth] by the [shorthand: hand] of our own free will and avow mutually acknowledge each other husband & wife in a covenant not to be broken in time or Eternity for time & for all Eternity, to all intents & purposes as though the seal of the covenant had been placed upon us, for time & all Eternity & called upon God, & all the Holy angels—& Sarah Long-th, to witness the same. Willard Richards, Sept. 1845-Feb. 1846 Diary, 23 Dec. 1845.

The question came up again in one of our subsequent Affirmation meetings and I again gave the same counsel as I had given that evening to George and Dean, "God, in all of Infinity's foreknowledge and mercy does not withhold any

181

blessing from those who are loving and desire the same blessings given to other loving couples. You who have any who love you, cling to them and thank God! Do as Willard Richards and Alice Longstroth did in 1845 when they found themselves without a person holding the Keys to function in the sealing power. Find a secluded, quiet place. Dedicate it for holy purposes with your Priesthood. Take one another by the hand, as you have been taught, and make a solemn covenant using the words Willard Richards did and covenant to be one another's 'companion' for time and all Eternity and keep a written record of it."

I've often thought of George and Dean since then. I had left them with a promise: "Someday, God will authorize that gay and lesbian couples be sealed as heterosexual couples can be sealed today. Until then, this method will witness your intent and God will not be blind to your love."

George responded, "That sounds nice Tony, but what makes you feel that such a covenant without a sealer exercising the sealing power would be sufficient in the eyes of God?"

"In my view, L.D.S gays, lesbians, and bisexuals are in the exact situation today as the polygamist faithful found themselves in the years immeadiately after the 1890 Wilford Woodruff Manifesto. The new and everlasting covenant is meant to be a universal one, for 'every people'. The scientific discoveries of Dr. Jan Stout and others now offer to all of us a glimmer of evidence that we are in a very real sense a 'people' distinguished from other peoples by our biological propensity to experience physical intimacy with those of our own kind. As with the faithful polygamous members of the Church in post-Manifesto Mormonism, you can take counsel from President George Q. Cannon. In the April 5, 1894 meeting of the First Presidency and the Twelve Apostles, he advised: *I believe in concubinage, or some plan whereby men and women can live together under sacred ordinances and vows until they can be married...*'"

George expressed shock at the idea that a member of the Church's First Presidency would suggest concubinage years after the Presidency had issued the Manifesto against such things.

Dean asked, "What is concubinage, anyway?"

"Webster's Dictionary defines concubinage as 'the living together of two persons as if they were husband and wife.'"

I'd discovered in my visit with George and Dean that day in Kansas City that I had a very definite opinion on just how I should respond to questions regarding the sacred power with which I'd been endowed.

The following week I met a psychology professor on campus. He was one of the psychology professors on campus who worked with self-mind control techniques. I established a friendship with him and one day I asked, "Would you teach me to control my tendency to bind myself by my self-inflicted guilt?"

"Well, Tony. It sounds like the battle's half won."

"How so?"

"You have already acknowledged in your conscious mind that the guilt you feel is self-inflicted. All we need to do is teach your subconscious mind to let your conscious mind take control on this one."

Several days later, after settling down in a comfortable overstuffed easy chair in his study, I said "Okay, I'm ready."

"Tony, psychologists are very conscious about an experiment known as the Milgram experiment, but persons of sensitivity hate to recall it to memory."

"Why is that?"

Then, he began to explain something to me that I've thought of rather frequently since those first sessions with him. "This now famous, or rather infamous, experiment was prompted by curiosity, a curiosity into how it is that ordinary people, who love just like you and I, will do such terrible things—truly abominable things—when authority orders it." He suddenly got very serious, his face was a blank stare as if he was seeing through mine, beyond me.

"Tony, It was a mirror of the Nazis who'd claimed as an excuse that they were 'only obeying orders' when confronted with their war atrocities."

As he said this, I remembered the scene from my days as a Mormon Bishop in Utah when President Farnsworth had said so easily to me "Remember, Tony, the President is right, even when he's wrong," and I suddenly became somber also.

"What is it, Tony?"

"That's exactly what a Mormon Stake President once said to me years ago."

"What, that he was 'only obeying orders'?"

"No. He was trying to get me to see that our simply 'obeying orders' was more important to God than to obey our conscience."

"The researcher," he continued, "took people into a room who were told they were going to take part in an experiment. A screen divided the room so that the person in the first half could hear, but not see, what was going on in the second half. The people in the first half were seated before the controls of a machine which they were told would administer electric shocks of increasing severity to a person in the second half on the room. This people actually believed that on the other side of the screen somebody sat strapped in to a chair and wired up to the shock machine. In reality, the people in the second half of the room sat before an indicator telling them how they should react to the *supposed* shocks they were receiving—first with grunts and groans, then with screams and terrified pleas begging the experimentors to stop, and finally in silence as though they were unconscious or dead.

My friend stopped talking. He had become visibly upset by what he was relating to me. I was becoming upset as well, but I could tell that I was only getting the idea of what he was trying to convey to me; he'd obviously experienced something very unpleasant that was affecting him as he related this story to me. "At the 285-volt level," he went on, "the supposed recipients of the shocks gave an agonized scream and became silent. The people administering what they believed were extremely painful, even leathal doses of electricity were under great stress," his voice became almost a whisper, "but they went right on doing it, right up to the maximum of 450 volts. Afterwards, most couldn't believe they were capable of such behavior."

He stopped talking again. This time the silence went on until I said, "Well, did any of them realize what they'd done?"

"Some said, 'Well, I was only carrying out instructions.'"

I remembered that common counsel from Mormon leaders to their followers: *The Bishop is right, even when he is wrong. Obey his counsel, and if he's wrong, you'll be blessed for your obedience to priesthood authority.* I'd realized that those of the Mormon Community, whose choices were founded in obedience to authority more than in personal conscience, were no different from the guinea pigs in the Milgram experiment.

My friend was obviously emotionally spent. And, after arranging for our next session, we said good-by.

In another session, he introduced me to a simple process of meditation wherein I would practice going into a relaxed state of mind, a place where I could visualize whatever scene I desired and where I could change my environment at will. In this process, I learned to somehow project myself into other places where my body was not. I could be lying down or sitting in a comfortable chair physically, but be acutely aware of another totally distinct and separate physical place.

I'd wanted to get rid of the guilt I had felt for so many years. I now knew in my heart, in my inner-self, that this was false guilt. I knew that it was self-inflicted because of my upbringing. Our job was to get my mind aligned with what my inner-self, my spirit, had discovered.

One day, he asked if I was ready to take a "quantum leap."

"Sure," I said. Then, for about ten minutes, he guided me in an experience I'll never forget. After getting into what we were now calling an "alpha" state, we went through

185

another exercise that projected me out of my body. He picked up a small audio tape cassette case, took out the cassette and closed the case up again.

"Have you ever seen this cassette case before, Tony?"

"No."

"Good. How would you like to get inside it?"

Suddenly, I was inside the cassette! It seemed crazy, but I actually could see everything around me as if I were inside the small cassette case!

He asked me what I saw.

I looked around me. "On the right, I see a large ball of orange yarn with yellow, brown, and darker orange specks in it."

"Where are your feet, Tony? Look down," he said.

Looking down, I could see that I was standing right on the edge of the black plastic with my toes hanging over the clear plastic part of the case. I verbalized my location.

"Do you see any scratches in the plastic, Tony?"

"No, I don't. Wait. I see lots of scratches on the clear plastic, but there aren't any at all on the black part of the case," I responded.

"Okay now, Tony, I want you to come out of the case." With that, I found myself back outside of the case and sitting where I had been before.

"Let yourself see the guilt you've been wearing for all these years as an old blanket that you have wrapped around your body." Again, it worked. I was covered by a blanket. It covered all of me, except for my head, as I sat in the chair.

"What color is it?"

"Black."

"Do you want to keep on wearing this guilt?"

"No."

"Then, why do you still have it wrapped around you?"

"I don't know."

"Tony, why don't you just take it off?" I then simply took off the old dark and heavy blanket that I had covering me. It was so simple. It was so easy to do.

186

"I took it off!"

"Good. Now, Tony, you'll keep it off. Won't you?"

"Yes."

He took me out of my alpha state. When I had totally come into this consciousness, he opened up the little audio cassette case for me to look inside. I was totally amazed by what we both saw. On one end, over in the corner, there was a small orange particle of lint. There were scratches all over the clear portion of the case with none on the black portion. The black part of the case had ridges in the corners which protected it from getting scratched.

"That was fantastic!"

"Tony, who put that guilt on you that you were carrying?"

"I did."

"Aren't you glad to know that since you are the one responsible for it, you can also take it off?"

"Oh, thank you!" Indeed. What my friend had just led me through was the experience that finally allowed me to synchronize my subconscious mind with my conscious mind. It'd allowed me to continue on in my efforts at becoming an integrated, whole person of healthy mind, spirit, and body.

"The best thanks you can ever give me, Tony," he said, "is to keep your spiritual telescope focused on those things that are cosmically or ultimately true."

"What do you mean?"

"Tony, in order for any religious theme to be true, it must be rooted in a cosmic context; otherwise, it's false religion. I believe that the guilt you had accepted as your own had its origin in a belief system focused in cultural considerations rather than cosmic vision. Remember, Tony, science has shown many times over that the most constant characteristic of the universe is unpredictability and that time and space are curved."

I stared back at him. I still didn't understand what he was trying to say.

187

"Tony, to say that something is 'unpredictable' is to own the fact that to us it is incomprehensible, that your way of conprehending does not apply here."

"But, what does that have to do with the bending of time and space in the universe?"

"Religious communities call incomprehensible things 'mysteries.' Like the scientists, they just accept their reality and also, like scientists, theologians vainly try to understand. When we see ourselves in light of ultimate or cosmic realities, we must be content to accept that contradictions in life need not be understood, but only experienced so that we may grow in them. When religious tradition tries to explain any given circumstance by our limited earth-bound vision, we end up with a blurred vision, at best. Our spiritual telescopes must be aimed and focused on cosmic principles. Only then in our acceptance of our inability to comprehend will we gain from life's realities."

Seeing that I still didn't totally understand what he was getting at, he encouraged me to return as often as I wanted. And I did return. Over and over again, he would remind me of his words. Once he told me not to worry, the meaning of his words would come to me. He would also remind me to constantly look for examples of forgiveness in my life and in the lives of those around me. He said that seeing these examples and acknowledging them as the way to live would help me to continue to forgive myself as life went on. I didn't have to look very far for examples...

Larry and Wes, two friends of mine from old B.Y.U. days, lived on the Kansas side of the river in Kansas City. We'd often visit one another socially. I sat in Larry's home, just across the river from the Park College campus. There had been a stream of stories in the news media about homocides and other brutal violent crimes. I was reading Larry's morning newspaper.

Coming Out Spiritually

"I couldn't ever kill another person," Larry said as I finished reading. "Could you?"

"No" I answered simply.

"No. I take that back" he corrected himself. "There was a time when I would have, but I just didn't know who the person was I wanted to kill."

I shook my head in disbelief.

"Well, you need to understand the circumstances, Tony. There really was a time when I could have killed another person."

"That's hard to believe." He'd always seemed such a mild, loving person.

Larry explained that when he was a senior at Brigham Young University in Provo, Utah, he'd been targeted in an investigation carried out by the campus Standards Office. Evidently Campus Security, backed by people from the Standards Office, had "suspect" students followed as they made the weekly 45 mile trip north from Provo to Salt Lake City to attend Affirmation meetings there.

After setting up a "stake out" outside the Affirmation meeting, the BYU Campus Security officers would record car license plate numbers. These would then be matched up with student records and the "suspect" students called into the campus Standards Office for questioning.

"But I never drove a car there, Tony," he said. "There was no way anyone could connect me to anything at Affirmation. I didn't even use my real name at the meetings. Actually, I didn't even know for sure back then if I was gay or not. I was just going to get information more than anything else."

"So how did you get found out?"

"I was eating at the 'Cougareat,' you remember it was the snack bar in the student union building? Anyway, one day a friend introduced me to two of his gay friends."

"But what does this have to do with wanting to kill someone?"

"Tony, one of those guys at the 'Cougareat,' or my roommate, had to be the one that turned me in. Nobody else

189

even knew that I was going to the Affirmation meetings in Salt Lake City."

"I don't know," I said shaking my head. "Somehow that doesn't really seem worth killing for. Just because they gave your name to the campus police."

"Tony, I had only one more semester left. The Standards Office wouldn't let me register for that last semester. I couldn't transfer more than half of my entire college credits. In order to graduate, I would practically have had to start college all over again. At the time, I felt like that person, whoever he was, had totally destroyed my life. I was violated, Tony! What kind of time do you think I had telling the story to my family? I did want to kill him."

The conversation turned to other things, and I sort of forgot about what Larry had said.

Two weeks later, however, another experience brought it vividly back to my mind. I was packing for a trip when Wes came by to give me a ride to the airport. Larry had arrived earlier to help and Wes watched Larry pack. After finishing my preparations, I joined the two of them in the study where they were looking over the manuscript of this book. They were joking and laughing.

As I entered the room, Wes grew suddenly somber. He set the typewritten pages on the desk and looked at me in a kind of panic, then he turned to Larry. He picked up the pages and then set them down again, as if he wished that whatever it was he was struggling so to say would be written there, and he could just hand it to Larry instead of having to say it aloud.

"I...I, uh, I have something I need to tell you, Larry," he said finally, speaking with some difficulty.

There was an awkward silence. "Hey, you guys, maybe I'd better leave you alone," I said, getting to my feet.

"No, Tony," Wes said firmly, "I want you here for this."

I sat back down.

Larry took Wes's hands in both of his, giving Wes security for whatever it was Wes was working so hard to express.

190

"Larry, I have something to confess to you." His eyes filled with tears, but he didn't move to brush them away. The tears just kept falling over his cheeks and onto their laps as they sat there in front of me.

"What?" Larry whispered, "What, Wes?" He sat without moving, Wes's hands clenched in his own.

Wes's voice cracked as he tried to speak. He swallowed and tried again, "Larry, do you remember when we first met?"

"Of course" Larry answered quickly. It was the meeting in the BYU Student Union Center that Larry had told me about, the meeting when he'd met two new gay guys at the Cougareat.

Wes took a deep breath, then spoke in a rush, as if he were afraid that if he paused at all he wouldn't be able to keep speaking. "I'm the person that turned you into the Standards Office. They forced me to do it. My Bishop said part of my repentance was to give him the names of all the guys I thought were gay. I believed him. He was my Bishop, Larry. I wanted to graduate. I only had one class left. I wanted to do the right thing. But all I did was hurt a lot of other people who'd never done anything to hurt me." He was pale.

Larry couldn't respond.

"I'm sorry," Wes repeated, "I'm sorry, Larry. Can you forgive me?"

Larry put his arms around Wes. "You really believed you couldn't repent unless you gave them every single name, didn't you?"

Wes nodded, still holding onto Larry, weeping bitterly, completely.

"Of course I forgive you, Wes," Larry said as he kept ahold, hugging Wes while all the pain of years of guilt began to lift from him. "I forgave you a long time ago. Please forgive yourself. You've been holding onto this agony for far too long now. Let it go." They sat there. Both of them weeping openly in front of me.

191

Out of the Bishop's Closet

I realized that I had witnessed a profound healing. It was a true synchronization of two who had been dischordant. It was a letting go by his mind of a sickness that it had forced upon his spirit. I thought of my psychologist friend on the faculty at Park College. I remembered his comments about not trying to understand in rational terms the "why" of situations, but to just accept their reality. In witnessing this healing of two of my friends, I had to admit that I didn't understand how the wounds had been healed in their interchange, but I could see that it was wonderful to see the eternal principle of forgiveness in action. Whatever the rational understanding of the principle of forgiving could be, for me, all I needed to comprehend was what I'd seen. I had witnessed its healing power.

During those same months at Park College, I would go over to Tim and his wife Cathy's home on a regular basis. They lived nearby in Liberty, Missouri, and frequently enjoyed each other's company. Knowing that my children were growing up, going through life's changes in another place away from me was, oftentimes, more than I could bear. It was during those kinds of times that I yearned to have my own boys and girls close to me. I needed a fatherly association with other children and Tim and Cathy's family was a great comfort to me.

My visits to their home in Liberty would sometimes linger on into the dawning hours of another day. Tim and I had always talked for hours whenever we'd get together, ever since our college days together. One night we began to talk about the Adam-God doctrine—an idea taught for twenty-five years by Brigham Young and all other Mormon Church leaders of that time with only one exception. It was a dogma that held that God himself had come to earth as the first man, and had been the literal father of our bodies, as well as of our spirits—that it had been Adam who'd fathered the body of Jesus, that Eve and Mary were both plural wives of "Father

Adam." It was a theology that had always left a strange taste inside of me. I'd expressed my observation that Mormon doctrine had been reconstructed since the 1890 Manifesto, that the Adam-God doctrine was just one example where the President of the Church had "led the people astray."

Tim was arguing, rather feebly, that doctrine changes, and that any who wouldn't accept the doctrine of the current Prophet over that of dead Prophets had "become prophets unto themselves." Tim went on saying, "Tony, changing doctrine is the nature of continuing revelation through the Prophets, the Presidents of the Church."

I looked at him sideways, raising one eyebrow. "Do you really believe that?"

"That doctrine can change? I'm not sure. It seems that if truth is eternal, then doctrines wouldn't change, but ..." His voice trailed off as he realized his own arguments didn't really make rational sense.

I stood up and began pacing rapidly back and forth across the floor, as if my feet were trying to keep up with my words. "That's how we know!" I exclaimed.

"Know what?"

"That the Prophets don't speak absolute or unchanging truth. If they did, their teachings would always be exactly the same, no matter what the time, society, culture, or circumstances of the people. But they can't separate themselves completely from their backgrounds, no matter how they try. Revelation from God, if it is to be shared, has to be put into language. And images and symbols and parables have to come from our daily experiences if we're going to understand at all."

"So, maybe," he said slowly, "even if everyone was a 'prophet unto himself' and what they were saying seemed to be contradictory, it wouldn't really be?"

"Sort of. But even more than that, those kinds of people are going to be open to truth from those around them, even if the words and the context and the way that truth comes is a little unfamiliar to them. They'll accept it because Prophets are, at heart, seekers after truth."

193

Tim pushed a stuffed bear off the couch and lay down, his hands behind his head. "It's a nice dream isn't it?"

"I told you about the General Conference of the Church where they accepted the Wilford Woodruff pronouncements?" I went on.

He nodded.

"Well, that's why that was so hard for me to accept. Why, in fact, I decided then that I just couldn't be committed to the Church anymore. Tim, do you see that by accepting those statements as scripture, they were saying that the leaders were infallible, and that what the leaders said was absolute, all the time?"

"Sort of like they didn't want any of the members to learn to be their own prophets."

"No. It wasn't 'sort of.' That's exactly what the leaders wanted. But the scriptures have always taught that we are all called to become '*a royal priesthood*,' each one of us with a perfected and individual clear channel opened up, connected to our God's Holy Spirit."

"That must have really hurt you, Tony. I remember the strong testimony you used to bear about your witness of the divine call that those men have as the Apostles and Prophets of the Church." Tim had been present in the Smith Fieldhouse on the BYU campus when I had spoken to a student devotional assembly and shared the experience I'd had years earlier with David O. McKay when I was only sixteen.

"Yes, Tim, I was terribly hurt. I felt as though my loyalty had been betrayed. And I couldn't forgive them for it."

"Do you think that you ever will be able to forgive?"

"I hope so. I guess so." I thought of Elder _____, of the Twelve Apostles in Salt Lake City, Utah. "I had to forgive myself first, Tim, before I could really forgive them."

Suddenly, I was filled with a desire to see the video of the Mormon General Conference that Tim and Cathy had made only a few months before. "Tim, would you put on the video of the last General Conference? I'm especially interested in the talk by Elder _____."

Coming Out Spiritually

"Isn't he the...?"

"Yes," I interrupted.

We watched the conference talk.

"My brothers and sisters," Elder _____ said as he closed his address, "I wish to leave you my witness of our Savior Jesus Christ. I bear you my special witness that He is The Christ. He is the Savior and Redeemer of us all—you and me." The words sounded in my ears, echoing and reverberating as if they came from far away.

My emotions broke. The man on the television screen was crying.

I remembered how I'd once cried openly in a fast and testimony meeting when I was a member of a Bishopric in a student ward at BYU. Later I'd asked my Bishop, Rodney Turner, why we sometimes get so overcome that we cry openly in these moments. His response was, "Tony, sometimes we cry because we're overcome by the Spirit and they're tears of joy. Other times, we feel deeply unworthy and they're tears of pain, inward pain because we know all too well how truly unforgiven we are of ourselves."

Watching this Apostle on the television screen weep openly as he expressed his special witness of the Savior, I felt such compassion, such love, such tender understanding for this man that I couldn't hold back my own tears. "I forgive you," I said in my mind.

Tim was watching me a little strangely, not sure if he should try to comfort me or leave me alone or what.

I turned to Tim. "I want to tell you something, Tim." I said, "I want you to know that I love that man." I'd learned again how good the men who lead the Mormon Church really are, at least in their heart of hearts. I'd worked with them. I'd known their sincere desires to do right, to lead the people correctly. Now, I could finally acknowledge it totally and completely. I could acknowledge their goodness as ministers for God along with acknowledging their humanity as my fellow travelers in this world of weaknesses.

Tim understood.

Out of the Bishop's Closet

We talked for quite some time later about love, forgiving, and the significance of self-love to forgiveness. At one point, Tim sat up and held out his arm for me to come over to him. I did. As he hugged me there on the living room sofa, I continued expressing the deepest feelings of my heart while the dawn of morning broke in the window behind us.

"In much the same way, we also need to become whole and complete before we can even try to give out to others. We need to allow for our own personal spiritual development before our opportunities to aid others can be fruitful for us. I AM is the Divine expression of the core principle of Eternity: Free Agency, the power of personal choice. As long as we abdicate that sovereignty to others, we cannot exercise personal conscience. Do you remember the Milgram experiment?"

Tim just silently nodded, still holding me in the warmth of his arms.

"That's *us*, Tim, each of us. *We* are at the controls of the political machine in this society. The machine that has simply accepted the instruction of our paternalistic churches on how to license marriages in our civil law. Tim, have you ever wondered why we don't allow gays to marry in this society?"

I saw tears well up in his eyes.

"Tim, there are so many who love just like you and Cathy love, but our laws are *"Forbidding to marry."* Until we allow personal conscience to speak louder than paternalistic leaders, we won't see that we are causing intense pain, suffering, and agony to our own who are with us in the same room. Until then, we won't listen to the groans, the screams, and the pleas of those on whom we continue to administer our own brand of electric shock treatment. Other people have placed a room divider between us—blinding us to the fact that we really are all one. They claim to be responsible as they dictate our actions and urge us to keep obedience. But the truth is, *we will be held responsible for our choices*. Each of us chooses how much we actually follow in the footsteps of Jesus

196

by our choices, and it is only our choices that we take with us beyond death. Jesus really did show us how to do this best."

Tim just listened to me. He didn't let go, he just let me talk.

"Jesus spent a great amount of his time alone. He lived His life with an almost inconceivable awareness of the complete connectedness of all that was both in Him and around Him. In this cosmic awareness, He acted in the very center of His life. There was an incredible harmony about all that Jesus did, and it existed in the profoundest simplicity. At any given moment, He did only what that moment required. He was calm, serene, centered, and clear; even while confusion and upheaval surrounded Him. He knew His place in the cosmic reality. He was completely cognizant of what He was about. John, the Apostle who was called "The Beloved of the Lord," teaches us beautifully and so eloquently that Jesus is the personification of love, unconditional love for himself and all else."

We sat there in each other's warmth, with our tears and our joy, for some time.

Tim was the first to break our silence. He began whispering, his voice cracking with emotion, "Tony, I feel that it's when we learn to love ourselves that all of our separate selves can finally become integrated. What is love, if it isn't an 'affinity for?' So it appears that our spiritual goal truly is one of unity, or coming together, and not just within ourselves, but among ourselves as well. Ultimately it's true for tall of Creation isn't it, Tony?"

We remained there in silence, doing what we could to seal the moment forever in our minds, knowing it was coming to an end.

Tim was a friend, indeed. He and his wife, Cathy, had been able to love me even when I hadn't loved myself. These people saw beyond the stereotype of what I was supposed to be. While we were very different in our ideologies, we saw ourselves in unity and love. I sometimes think it was that kind of love that prepared me to take the steps to finally love myself. And by loving myself, I was able to forgive myself; then that forgiveness could flow out from me toward all whom I'd felt hurt me in the past.

It was my second year at Park College. Tim and Cathy had moved to the Chicago, area and I had made friends with a good group of people both on and off campus. I had been instrumental in organizing a local chapter of Affirmation, and I had grown personally through the love and tender watchcare of others. Many of my questions had been answered; many had not. But, the need to have all the answers had vanished from me. I had begun to live in the moment.

I received word through a friend that Garry Milner had been diagnosed with AIDS. He was planning to die peacefully in his San Fernando Valley home in California with his life's companion and his son. I decided to write him a letter.

Garry had encouraged me to move to Missouri after I'd been aided out of my suicidal depression by Chad. I wanted to return the loving care to Garry which he'd always given to others. I'd only been one of many to whom Garry had extended himself in true brotherhood when he was the Los Angeles Chapter Director for Affirmation. He'd listened for many long hours to me when I was confused, frightened, recently excommunicated, and divorced.

We'd met years before, though.

Garry had been serving as the Elder's Quorum President in the L.D.S. Ward near the Los Angeles Temple when Laura and I lived in that area years before our stay in Utah. When I was called to serve as a Stake High Councilor, I heard of Garry's faithful labors in Priesthood service through the other members of the High Council. His name often came up as a shinning example of excellent Priesthood leadership. Later, when I was reassigned as the President, or pastor, of the Spanish-speaking branch of the Church in that Stake, I got to know Garry from personal experience in Church work that involved us both.

Coming Out Spiritually

Among other thoughts, I wrote this:

Dear Garry,
...I have learned to see that there are only a few
absolutes. I now see that the principle of dynamic change is as
absolute as any. There is always change. Our various parts
(mind, spirit and body) are in constant change just like
anything else in the universe. These are dynamic entities. Our
various selves are in constant motion, either expanding in our
development or retracting in our retardation. Our efforts at
synchronization of mind, spirit and body are successful to the
degree that we can get all three to continue on together in
perfect dynamic union "through, with and in" each other at
the same velocity and in the same direction....

When I found out you'd been diagnosed, I pondered all
the wonderfully good things you've given me to keep for the
rest of my lives. Our choices, after all, are the only things we
actually take with us beyond this life as individuals. I am
eternally grateful for your wisdom, Garry. I can finally see
that it's through my choices that synchronization of mind,
spirit and body come to be.

I'm sure you've thought much about death lately.
Since I was once in a suicidal frame of thinking, I have also
thought much about what death is and what it isn't. I've come
to the realization that, if we're past our adolescent years,
we're in the process of physical death. We are all dying as far
as our bodies are concerned, our cells are not reproducing
themselves faster than they die off. To me, someone with AIDS
is different from me, only in the sense that they know how they
will probably finally die and approximately when, give or take
a few years. I could easily die in an accident on a crowded
freeway today. You could, in fact, outlive me. It's only the odds
that say you won't.

I have had to do a lot of letting go in the past few years.
In my yielding to God, I have discovered that there is hope that
springs from Eternity which allows me to see with my spiritual
eyes that there is more than what we see and know by our

199

physical eyes and other senses. I've experienced things that make me consciously aware of my very real existence in (at least) three different dimensions simultaneously. This is something that I can only speak or write of, I cannot find words to clearly express what I've known.

There is a completeness of life that continues after death and it's where we came from when we were born into this world. Our life on this plane of existence is only a kind of holography. Mortality is like a projection of what is real and that reality vibrates out to us from its other dimensions not confined by time and space. Our physical selves are composed in coarser vibrations so that the Eternal forrest (so to speak) is made opaque by the trees of time and space. If that weren't so, Garry, I fear some of us would choose to leave this world before we were ready. Our leaving would then be a curse rather than a blessing...

Some of my peace came through your suggestion to come out to Missouri when the opportunity arose for me to do so. As a result, today my desired spiritual destination is set on The Christ, The Heir of God. My spiritual path is now what I like to call "Zen Mormonism". Zen Mormonism is, to me, the centering of one's whole self—mind, spirit and body. It is the practice of eternal principles. My spiritual vehicle is The Holy Priesthood in all of its fullness of keys of knowledge. On this journey, Garry, I am not a passenger only. I am the driver. Others are prophets in the role of guides, but I alone, am at the wheel of my vehicle on this spiritual pilgrimage...

Thank you, Garry, for being a person who has integrated self enough to love others in their suffering, in spite of their being different. It has been a blessing to have known you here. I would feel it an honor to find myself around you again. God bless!

Tony

I didn't ever find out if Garry received the letter, but I was told about his passing a couple of months after I mailed it. Garry Milner passed into transition while in company of both his son and his life's companion just as he'd wanted.

I stayed with the college only one more term before returning to California. My work there had been very fruitful. I had seen almost six semesters of seniors leave the campus for a commencement of their various lives. As Director of Residential Life, I had counseled many young people who were just beginning their lives. There were many people, especially young men in the men's residence halls, who'd sought out my counsel as word had gotten around that I would not condemn their sexual experimentation. College years are those times when young people are experimenting in all aspects of adult life. It's the time of growth into manhood and womanhood that lends itself best to responsible educational exploration. As I endeavored to assist these young people in seeing the choices they had in their lives, while neither condemning their experimentation nor promoting it, I was amazed to realize what I'd learned about myself in the process, and how hard some of those lessons had come.

One day, as I was packing up my office in the Student Union Building and preparing to leave, I found myself listing all the things I'd learned in the years since I'd left my call as Bishop in Sandy, Utah so long ago...

I had learned that I am gay, after all. And I now knew that in spite of all the effort, energy, and striving I'd exerted to change myself into a heterosexual "head of household" in the Mormon tradition, I was still gay. Once, almost all of me had fit into the grand puzzle of life that Mormonism had been for me. My sexuality ,however, was an undeniable part of me that did not fit. The Church had told me that my sexuality was a perversion, that it was brought on by my sinful choices in mortality. The Church had taught me that I was ugly, evil, and wicked because of it. The Church had said that I should ignore it and suppress it, that I should repent of it and pray to be

201

delivered from it; and that if I did this long enough, and hard enough, it would eventually go away, and I could then be whole. But I had learned that it was only with my sexuality, together with the rest of me, that I could ever hope to become whole. True spirituality would have me welcome and incorporate all aspects of myself to become whole. It was only institutional religiosity that demanded that I dissect myself and slice out pieces here and there in order to fit into their particular version of godliness. True religion would have me acknowledge all of me, including my homosexual physical reality, as a gift of nature, an endowment from God.

I had learned that the Kinsey Reports, initiated in 1948, began today's scientific understanding of homosexuality. Kinsey developed a scale called the "Homosexual-Heterosexual Component" which consisted of ratings of one to six: one being exclusively heterosexual and six being exclusively homosexual. The Kinsey Reports revealed that, during a period of three years or more past the age of fifteen, 20% of American males fall into one of the last four categories: (#3) Equal homosexual and heterosexual arousal and experience, (#4) Largely homosexual orientation, (#5) Predominance of homosexual arousal arousal and experience, and (#6) Exclusively homosexual arousal and experience. Kinsey revealed some other surprising data: 38% of American males have at least one homosexual experience to orgasm during or after adolescence; of American males who remain single until their mid-thirties, 50% have had such experiences; a minimum of 12% of American males experience erotic attraction after adolescence to other males in the absence of any overt homosexual experience.

I had learned that in the German Democratic Republic, Dr. Ernst Dorner, director of experimental endocrinology at Humboldt University in East Berlin, believed homosexuals are products of maternal androgen deficiency, a lack of masculinizing hormones during a critical period of fetal brain development. Dr. Dorner's research had been confirmed in separate research conducted by Brian A. Glade of the Program in Human Sexuality at North Dakota State University and by Richard Green, director of the Program in Psychiatry, Law, and Human Sexuality at U.C.L.A. The governments of East Germany and New Zealand cited Dorner's studies as sufficient reason to decriminalize homosexuality in those nations. In fact, East Germany provided state-funded social organizations and legal protection for its homosexual citizens.

I had learned that (not to be outdone) the state of Utah had in Dr. Jan Stout, assistant clinical professor of psychiatry at the University of Utah School of Medicine, another voice joining those of other scientific heralds of a new vision of homosexuality. Dr. Stout's research declared the clinical probability that a consistent minimum of 10% of American males have a biological propensity for sexual fulfillment other than as heterosexuals. (see Sunstone Theological Symposium, Stout, Dr. Jan, *"Sin and Sexuality: Psychobiology and the Development of Homosexuality,"* August 23, 1985, Salt Lake City, UT.) Dr. Stout's findings, along with those of the other scientists, had confirmed to me the wisdom of Joseph Smith in his comments in 1842 that *"the children of the kingdom"* should receive *"revelation...according to the circumstances in which [they] are placed."*

I had learned to view gender or sex (in contrast to sexuality) in a totally different way than I did before those lunch hours in the Church archives in Salt Lake City. Joseph Smith had shown that women and men were equals in the fullest sense. He had, in fact, championed the priestly role of woman by ordaining his wife Emma Hale Smith and by supervising the ordination of other women in 1842. But his attitude toward women had been completely overturned by the present day church which claimed him as its founder. In the words of one former Mormon woman, now feminist, *"Women have become the oppressed and exploited majority in the church."* The patriarchy of twentieth century Mormonism was certainly no longer my idea of godliness.

I had learned that, indeed, *"no unclean thing can enter the kingdom of God."* However, I had finally become enlightened enough to know that the real uncleanliness spoken of here are those things that cloud and darken an otherwise clear and pure vessel. It is not disobedience to some specific regulation, policy, or administrative procedure of a given church that causes us, as vessels of God's Spirit, to become unclean. Purity of heart has to do with being imbued with the principles of love of self, love of others and love of all. Purifying the vessel is done by acquiring those principles within our lives that reach into eternity. All the other commandments quoted by well-intentioned church leaders are only footnotes about the Law of God, at best. God *is* Love, after all.

I had learned that it is good to take theological positions, but those positions must be taken with humility, with openess of mind, and a willingness to learn more. I had discovered that my actions in life, while based on my beliefs, must be ever ready to adjust as new truth is given. Indeed, I had learned to bear the sweet burden of uncertainty.

I had learned that the path of spirituality is an aesthetic odyssey rather than a logically mapped-out highway. Our spiritual journey is not one that others can accurately prescribe for us so that we can get the way "down pat" beforehand. Others can only point us toward The Holy. We must be drawn unto that which is Holy by our own individual communion with The Divine. Jesus had given us the example showing how to travel, but we are still obliged to actually travel our own road. The only Sure Guide on that road is the Holy Ghost. What others hold out to us, claiming to be absolute truth, is unavoidably tainted by their own experience and influenced by their particular culture and society. This is true even for Prophets of God.

Thus, I had learned that Mormonism is not the only true spiritual path. While I still knew that, for me, Mormonism (as Joseph Smith had taught it) lifted up some essential truths that no other world religious philosophy contained in such clarity, I also knew that the wisdom, power and truth that lead us to The Infinite can be found in many other places as well.

Coming Out Spiritually

This same wisdom, power, and truth is found in all religions; it is simply expressed in different language and symbols. Over and over again, I had been reminded of the statement *"All truth may be circumscribed into One Great Whole."* The principles of eternity, I had learned, remained the same no matter which religious orientation or scientific discovery embodied them.

I had learned that the Church is a vehicle only. Its purpose is to help us along our spiritual path. But the vehicle cannot be more important than road we travel or the destination we seek. And when we discover it's no longer helping us to progress, it must be left behind.

I had learned that the church is, in reality, *the people who believe in God.* And when that people forget to love and otherwise follow in the footsteps of Jesus, they are no longer the true people or "church" of God. What makes a true people of God is what the word "true" actually means: to be exact and honorable. I remembered temple ceremonies had taught me that *"exactness and honor"* manifest that which is Godly in us. In order to be a true church or *people of God*, we would have to have acquired exactness and honor in manifesting godliness toward one another, beginning with ourselves. The true people of God would consistently endeavor—more than anything else—to measure up *"to the stature of the fullness of Christ."*

I had learned that it is in the doing that we grow, but that the goal is not merely to do. The real and essential goal is to *"get the Spirit"* by being willing to let go and yield ourselves to God. Again, I remembered the words of Joseph Smith when he reportedly returned in spirit form after his death, *"Tell the saints to get the Spirit of God."* The important message which he brought back was not to obey a particular commandment of Mosaic Law or some administrative policy of an institutional Church, but simply to *"get the Spirit of God."* As we learn to do this, a true motivation, one that is complete in its exactness and honor, will enter our being, and the doing will be a natural result.

Out of the Bishop's Closet

I had learned that Joseph Smith had written that the highest good *"consists in obtaining the powers of the holy priesthood"* and also that *"Zion cannot be built up unless it is by the principles of the law of the celestial kingdom..."* The "powers of the holy priesthood" are indeed "the principles of the law of" heaven. We are not in heaven yet, thus, the law itself is unknowable to us. However, the principles of the law of heaven which are manifest to us in this world are within our grasp. As we obtain them, clarity of soul, purity of heart, and centeredness of being become natural to us.

I had learned what Joseph Smith tried to teach when he wrote: *"care not for the body, neither the life of the body; but care for the soul and the life of the soul"*. For Joseph had earlier defined what he meant by the word "soul" in saying: *"...the spirit and the body are the soul ..."* To Joseph,` then, the soul was not what most people would call a spirit; it was not some amorphous, nonphysical vapor that dwells inside a human body; it was, rather, both the body and the spirit together. Joseph also wrote, *"spirit and element, inseparately connected, receive a fullness of joy."* So, in caring "for the soul and the life of the soul" Joseph was speaking of the need to bring together both body and spirit in such a unified and perfect way that they can ultimately receive complete joy. That's why he also wrote, *"...the resurrection from the dead is the redemption of the soul."* In other words, the Holy Resurrection is the redemption, the "bringing back into original beingness" of the spirit and the body. I'd learned that this applied to my homosexual body as well as to those of others.

Thus, the grand objective of living, I submit to us all, is not to conquer nor subjugate the body to the will of the spirit, nor to ignore the spirit's wisdom and sensitivity as we appeas the body's desires. It is, rather, to *synchronize* both the spirit and the body—to have them flow in harmony with one another, moving in unison, without contention, toward their ultimate goal: godliness. This, I believe, is the business of mortal life, and in the Holy Resurrection, in that moment of Infinite sealing as part of The Divine, *"the whole"* will indeed become *"spiritual and immortal, that they may no more see corruption"*—**Mind, Spirit, and Body.** This is the understanding that has given rhyme and reason to my entire experience of coming out of the Bishop's closet.

Neither life nor death,
Neither wickedness in high places,
Neither things past nor things present,
Neither AIDS nor ARC,
Neither hate in the hearts of those who fear us,
Nor accusations of those who fear they are us,
Will ever keep us from the love of ourselves, each
other, and God —
Fully respondent to God's call to truly come Home,
Clean and dressed in our beautiful garments,
Prepared in Fullness for our Wedding Feast,
With the Bridegroom,
The Firstborn of Heaven!

adapted by the Author
from Romans 8: 38-39

Epilogue

After his excommunication in 1973, Sergio committed suicide. His aunt was the President of our Women's Relief Society and let me know when I visited Los Angeles in 1981 that his suicide note mentioned his excommunication as the major reason.

Pepe Gomez moved from Northern Chile, where we had baptized him, to Rio de Janeiro, Brazil. He is happy with his life's companion. They've been together since 1968 and have been living together in Brazil since then. His wife, Chica, died of a heart attack before he moved away.

The Bishop who gave me the assignment to spy on the polygamists in Salt Lake City, Utah, was made the Stake President of his Stake. He is active in Salt Lake City's politics.

According to a fellow ex-member of our ward near the Utah State Capitol, Jim Bastewort was placed in the Utah State Mental Hospital in Provo, Utah, through the efforts of two social workers.

Jared Thurston married two additional wives. His family continues to grow and prosper.

President Farnsworth served as Stake President until 1987. He was replaced by his counselor. The new Stake President is the realtor who assisted Laura in selling our home in Sandy, Utah.

Steve, my counselor in the Bishopric of the Sandy ward was made Bishop and Rick, my other counselor in the same ward, was called to the Stake High Council.

When I visited the Ward on Easter Sunday in 1987 because a friend was singing in the ward choir for the Easter program, my friend was privately informed by her Bishop that I would "be physically removed from the chapel" should I ever return to their church meetinghouse. Ultimately, my friend was forced to sell her home in their Ward because of the persecutions her children received from peers in the Ward membership and the hate mail she received from her fellow Mormon neighbors.

In 1982, I began to search out those individuals I had personally had any part of excommunicating or disfellowshipping from the church because of their homosexual or bisexual activity. By the end of 1985, I had been able to locate all of those still alive and I personally apologized for my incorrect decision regarding their membership in the Church. In every case, their response was one of love and genuine compassion.

Dr. James O. Mason left his employment at the Church Offices some months after the dissolution of the department he headed. He is now the Director of the Centers for Disease Control (C.D.C.) in Atlanta, Georgia. I frequently see him on the news media as he reports on the A.I.D.S. epidemic in this country.

During a lecture tour of California, I found M. Dale Hansen alive and well. Our meeting was joyous as neither of us had expected to find the other again. He said, "Mostly, I'm happy seeing how different you are now, compared to the guilt-ridden person you were in 1980." I had been right. It was my tremendous guilt complex in those days that had caused him to avoid me. We now see one another, as friends, as often as our two paths cross. His operation was a success and he's very happy remodeling an old Victorian home he recently purchased in Sacramento, California.

When I was on the Religious Advisory Board of AIDS PROJECT LOS ANGELES, I frequently received calls from persons with AIDS and ARC who had requested an opportunity to receive spiritual counseling from a Mormon gay person. One Sunday, as I prepared to go to a church service, Jason Adams called on the telephone. He had decided to contact me when he saw my name listed in the APLA directory. Jason told me that his lover of three years had died of AIDS only three months earlier and that he had been diagnosed with the same disease just days before he'd called me. We both expressed our joy at finding each other again and we agreed to visit. I tried to visit him several times, but his family would not allow us to see each other. I have not heard from him since.

The last time Bill Detton and I sat down reminiscing about our days in Hollywood, California, we confronted a very sensitive subject. I had introduced Bill and Gregg Alda. After Gregg had moved into the apartment Bill and I had shared, they developed into a warm and loving couple. Slightly over a year thereafter, Gregg died suddenly from complications developed from hepatitis B. Bill is now comfortably set in the commercial real estate business in southern California. He has been in a monogamous relationship with his life's companion since 1983.

After hearing through the grapevine that his former Bishop had "come out of the closet," Jeff contacted me by telephone and let me know that he and Irene had gotten divorced because he'd come out of his closet again. Jeff had met a returned Mormon missionary in 1983 and they've been together since. When he came out, those accustomed to gossip in our old ward spread false rumors that he'd been involved with me in an affair when I was their Bishop. We both had a good laugh at their mistaken assumptions about us.

Chad replaced me as Director of Personnel at Hughes Aircraft Company. He is now a Vice President of Human Resources Management for a financial institution in southern California. Chad's companion of three years died in 1987.

Carl Solani moved to Phoenix, Arizona and founded the Phoenix Chapter of Affirmation, Gay and Lesbian Mormons. Last I heard, he was active in the political arena of Arizona state government.

Tim and Cathy now have eight children and Tim is active in his ward in the Chicago area again as Elder's Quorum President. They remain genuine and loving Latter Day Saints as they rear an exemplary family.

My friend Ron in Kansas City, Missouri, encouraged those I had worked with in our Affirmation, Kansas City Chapter, to organize themselves into what has now become GAY AND LESBIAN ALLIANCE, the social and support group for gays and lesbians in the Reorganized Church of Jesus Christ of Latter Day Saints. Since most of them were members of the Reorganized Church, this has resulted in some notable success.

Dean and George solemnized their union as I'd suggested to them. They're still together and are an example of how all married couples can grow closer and more loving in their relationship with the passage of time. They've since adopted a child and they are very happy as the proud parents of a little boy that they are raising as a Roman Catholic.

After his experience with the Holy Priesthood in what seems to have been a rather miraculous healing of a person with AIDS, Luke's surviving Lover involved himself as a volunteer with his local AIDS Shanti Foundation. His work with Shanti is very rewarding for him and allows him to share his great capacity to love others by being there when they are in need.

Burt continues to conduct his personal historical research into the actual identity of the "vary friend" of Lorenzo D. Barnes in the Salt Lake City headquarters of the L.D.S. Church. At the time of printing, he'd discovered that President Wilford Woodruff (the Mormon President who stopped the sealing of men to men in 1894 by saying that Brigham Young had "changed the ordinance" and that "more revelation [was] needed" before continuing its practice) had a woman by the name of Isabella Pratt and her children from two previous marriages sealed posthumously to Lorenzo D. Barnes on October 9, 1895. The sealing record indicates that Lorenzo D. Barnes had been "a single man without any previous marriage." The Apostle who had visited the grave of Lorenzo D. Barnes in England in 1845 evidently saw to it that Lorenzo D. Barnes had a family sealed to him *after* this same Apostle had, as President of the Church, stopped the practice of sealing men to men.

It was rather curious to me, to hear from Burt that subsequent pages of the *Wilford Woodruff Journal* indicate that the "Lover" of Lorenzo D. Barnes was a woman named Susan Conrad whom President Woodruff then called the "intended" of Lorenzo Barnes. Seeing this, raised even more questions: Why wasn't this term used by Joseph Smith, Willard Richards, and Wilford Woodruff himself when speaking or writing in Nauvoo about this person? Also, if the "Lover" of Lorenzo D. Barnes was only an "intended" or engaged woman at the time of Lorenzo's death, why did President Woodruff indicate by his personal shorthand-like code that this "Lover" was Lorenzo's "priesthood Lover", or "kingdom Lover," or "sealed Lover?" Burt has reported to me that he has been unable to identify any person in Nauvoo records of the time by the name of Susan Conrad other than this statement by Wilford Woodruff in his journal entry of 1845. It remains for historians to uncover the type of relationship that actually existed between Lorenzo D. Barnes and his "vary friend" who was called the "priesthood or kingdom or sealed Lover" by the man who stopped the sealing of men to men over fifty years later. The key to this will be the true identity of the "vary friend" of Lorenzo D. Barnes.

Just prior to publication, Burt shared a note written by Lyndon Cook on *Doctrine and Covenants*, Section 131 in his book *The Revelations of The Prophet Joseph Smith*. In this note, Mr. Cook also mentions that the parenthetical statement had been added and "was not in the original." In the notes on Section 130, Mr. Cook makes reference to the fact that the Church Historians "modified" the *Manuscript History of The Church* so that verse 22 now reads as it does, but that neither the draft of *Manuscript History of The Church* nor the *William Clayton Journal* contain what is now scripture.

Burt and I continue to discuss Lorenzo Barnes. "Such historical data, however stimulating," I said later to Burt, "is not as powerful to me as what is in the already published scripture of the L.D.S. Church *(Doctrine and Covenants* 131—omiting the added parenthetical statement—and 132:6-7 & 48) together with the recorded statements of Joseph Smith. As far as Lorenzo D. Barnes, we can only speculate on the identity of the person with whom he shared an intimate relationship in Nauvoo prior to his mission to England. What is given as President Wilford Woodruff's testimony on that identity in his journal entry of 1845, needs to be seen in the context of the disguised relationships of his days in Nauvoo (which joined the reconstructed sealing theologies he later initiated). These disguised relationships in Nauvoo are a manifestation of the secret attitudes and identities which predominated the lives of the leaders in the 1840's in Nauvoo."

Laura and the children moved from California to Utah. She is currently employed by a subsidiary corporation of The Church of Jesus Christ of Latter-day Saints. The children are being raised as active members of the Church. I agreed with Laura when we divorced that, while I don't agree with the church in some areas, our children should be raised as active Latter Day Saints in the Church. Should the day come when they need to supplement what the church can provide them, I will stand equally ready to assist in love to create the environment necessary for them to continue on their own spiritual journey.

I followed through with my plan to move to California. I am now residing in San Francisco and continue to learn and grow in the great adventure that life has become for me.

Suggested Reading

The Male Couple's Guide to Living Together, by Eric Marcus, Harper and Row, New York, NY. 1988

The Male Couple: How Relationships Develope, by David P. McWhirter and Andrew M Mattison, Prentice Hall, New York, NY. 1985

The New Loving Someone Gay, by Donald H. Clark, Ph.d., Celestial Arts, Berkeley, CA. 1987

Good-bye, I Love You, by Carol Lynn Pearson, Jove Books, New York, NY. 1988

Man To Man, by Dr. Charles Silverstein, William Morrow & Co., New York, NY. 1981

Is The Homosexual My Neighbor?, by Letha Scanzoni & Virginia Mollenkott, Harper & Row, San Francisco, CA. 1978

Christianity, Social Tolerance And Homosexuality, by John Boswell, University of Chicago Press, Chicago, IL. 1980

Gay American History, by Jonathan Katz, Crowell, New York, NY. 1976

Prologue: An Examination of The Mormon Attitude Towards Homosexuality, Brigham Young University, Provo, UT. (only available through AFFIRMATION, GAY AND LESBIAN MORMONS)

Good News For Modern Gays, by Sylvia Penington, Lambda Christian Fellowship, P.O. Box 1967, Hawthorne, CA. 90250

The Church And The Homosexual, by John J. McNeil, Beacon Press, Boston, Mass. 1988 (Third Edition)

AIDS, The Spiritual Dilemma, by John Fortunato, Harper & Row, San Francisco, CA. 1987

On Death And Dying, by Elizabeth Kubler-Ross, Macmillan Publishing Co., New York, NY. 1969

Now That You Know, What Every Parent Should Know About Homosexuality, by Betty Fairchild & Nancy Hayward, Harcourt, Brace Jovanovich, New York, NY. 1979

But Lord They Are Gay, A Christian Pilgrimage, by Sylvia Penington, Lambda Christian Fellowship, P.O. Box 1967, Hawthorne, CA. 90250